SLOW COOKER

GOOD
HOUSEKEEPING

SLOW COOKER

QUICK-PREP RECIPES

★ GOOD FOOD GUARANTEED ★

HEARST BOOKS
New York

HEARST BOOKS
New York

An Imprint of Sterling Publishing
1166 Avenue of the Americas
New York, NY 10036

ISBN 978-1-61837-178-2

GOOD HOUSEKEEPING

Jane Francisco
EDITOR IN CHIEF
Melissa Geurts
DESIGN DIRECTOR
Susan Westmoreland
FOOD DIRECTOR
Sharon Franke
FOOD APPLIANCES DIRECTOR

Cover Design: Chris Thompson and Yeon Kim
Interior Design: Yeon Kim
Project Editor: Andrea Lynn

The Good Housekeeping Cookbook Seal guarantees that the recipes in this cookbook meet the strict standards of the Good Housekeeping Research Institute. The Institute has been a source of reliable information and a consumer advocate since 1900, and established its seal of approval in 1909. Every recipe has been triple-tested for ease, reliability, and great taste.

For information about custom editions, special sales, and premium and corporate purchases, please contact Sterling Special Sales at 800-805-5489 or specialsales@sterlingpublishing.com.

Distributed in Canada by Sterling Publishing
c/o Canadian Manda Group, 165 Dufferin Street
Toronto, Ontario, Canada M6K 3H6
Distributed in Australia by Capricorn Link (Australia) Pty. Ltd.
P.O. Box 704, Windsor, NSW 2756, Australia

Manufactured in China

2 4 6 8 10 9 7 5 3 1

www.sterlingpublishing.com

CONTENTS

Cajun Surf 'n' Turf Stew
(page 36)

Foreword

Wish you could walk into your house after a day of work and smell dinner already cooking? Done! Enter the slow cooker. Say goodbye to hectic weeknight dinner prep. With minimal morning (or even the night before) prep and one-pot cleanup afterwards, a few ingredients thrown into the crock become a piping hot dinner, often with leftovers included.

Slow Cooker provides everything needed for low-fuss, healthy recipes that keep dinner simple. The chapters are divided into Pasta, Poultry, Beef, Pork and Lamb, plus Vegetarian and Sides. Whatever you're craving, it's here, along with sidebars on slow-cooking desserts and a primer on what helps turn leftovers into new meals.

Poultry comes to the dinner rescue with Caribbean Chicken Thighs, Chicken Scarpariello, or Tex-Mex Chicken Soup. Move beyond ground beef with Ropa Vieja, our Latin-style shredded flank steak, or turn chuck roast into pulled Philly-Style Beef Sandwiches. Amp the flavors of meatless meals with African Sweet Potato–Peanut Stew or White Chili with Black Beans.

Then there are the recipes that go into the slow cooker "Who knew?" category. You may never go back to a more laborious technique after our Vegetarian Lasagna recipe. No more hovering over the stovetop with Butternut Squash Barley Risotto. Surprise the kids by cooking spaghetti noodles directly in the slow cooker, as in the Southwestern Chicken Stew.

Yet slow cooking isn't just for set-it-and-forget-it family dinners. Utilize it to create company masterpieces like Red Wine-Braised Short Ribs, Chicken Fricassee, or Tuscan Pork with Fennel. Even summer get-togethers need not rely on the grill. Choose from 3-Napkin Baby Back Ribs, Tangy BBQ Chicken, or Pulled Pork Sandwiches.

In the *Good Housekeeping* Test Kitchens our team develops, triple-tests, and, yes, tastes every recipe that carries the *Good Housekeeping* name. For this book we tested to make sure recipes work in any slow cooker, with any brand of ingredients, no matter what . . . And if your slow cooker gets a workout from this cookbook—well, we've got you covered with recommendations for new ones. So what are you waiting for? Delicious, no-fuss dinners await.

SUSAN WESTMORELAND
Food Director, *Good Housekeeping*

Introduction

THE SKINNY ON SLOW COOKING

Succulent meat and simmering suppers are at your disposal thanks to a slow cooker. Follow these tips to be certain you get the most from yours.

- Less tender cuts of meat and poultry—such as pork and lamb shoulder, chuck roast, beef brisket, and poultry legs—are best suited for slow cooking. Skim fat from cooking liquid when done.
- Fish and other seafood are not a good fit unless they are added in the last hour of cooking.
- Avoid using ground meat; its texture is compromised by long, slow cooking, resulting in a mealy, spongy quality.
- Slow cooking tends to intensify flavorful spices and seasonings such as chili powder and garlic, so use them conservatively. Dried herbs may lesson in flavor, so adjust seasonings at the end of cooking. If you're using fresh herbs, save some to toss in at the last minute for best flavor.
- For richer flavor in stews, sprinkle meat and poultry with flour and brown in skillet before slow cooking. Scrape up browned bits in skillet and add to the pot to help thicken sauce and enhance flavor.
- For even cooking, fill slow cooker bowl at least halfway, but never to the brim. For soups and stews, leave about 2 inches of space between food and lid.
- When you're cooking root vegetables, put them at the bottom of the pot—they cook at a slower pace than the meat.
- If your recipe produces more liquid than you want, remove solids with a slotted spoon to a serving dish and keep warm. Transfer liquid to a saucepan and cook on High, uncovered, to reduce to desired thickness.
- Most recipes can be prepped the night before—all you have to do in the morning is toss in ingredients and flip the switch on the slow cooker! Pre-measure ingredients, precut vegetables, trim meats, and mix liquids and seasonings. Refrigerate components separately in bowls or self-sealing plastic bags.

GET THE MOST FROM YOUR SLOW COOKER

BROWNING MEAT BOOSTS FLAVOR

Sautéing meats in a skillet (or in the slow cooker's insert if it's stovetop-safe) to achieve a golden-brown crust before programming the cook time will give your braise or stew heartier flavor.

KEEP THE LID CLOSED

When slow cookers lose heat, it takes them a long time to gain it back. Don't remove the lid until you have to. You don't need to check—we promise the food is cooking.

PLAY AROUND WITH TEMPERATURE AND TIME SETTINGS

Your kitchen might not be a chemistry lab, but a little experimentation may be necessary to get the best results. Try out a few combinations of temperature settings and cooking times to get a recipe just right.

USE THE RIGHT SETTING

If your meat is consistently overcooked, try reducing either the setting or the cooking time. It's also possible that your cooker's keep warm setting operates at too high a temperature. If you routinely keep food warm for 30 minutes or longer, reduce the time your recipe cooks before going into warm mode.

Tangy BBQ Chicken (page 33)

INTRODUCTION

More Uses for Your Slow Cooker

The slow cooker isn't just a dinner helper; look for it to lend a hand for breakfast, dessert, and a hot-simmered beverage.

OVERNIGHT OATMEAL SENSATION:

Breakfast from the slow cooker? Yep. Just add steel-cut oats before bedtime, and you'll wake up to a hot, creamy breakfast as healthy as it is hands-off. The simple how-tos: Spray 4- to 6-quart slow cooker bowl with nonstick cooking spray. To bowl, add **4 cups water, 2 cups low-fat (1 percent) milk, 1½ cups steel-cut oats,** and **¼ teaspoon salt**; stir to combine. Program to cook for 4 hours on Low and 4 hours on Warm. Makes about 5 cups. Serves 4.

....

EACH SERVING: ABOUT 275 CALORIES, 12G PROTEIN, 47G CARBOHYDRATE, 5G TOTAL FAT (1.5G SATURATED), 6G FIBER, 0MG CHOLESTEROL, 200MG SODIUM.

COCONUT RICE PUDDING

In 4½- to 6-quart slow cooker bowl, **add 2¾ cups water** with **¾ cup long-grain white rice; 1 (15-ounce) can cream of coconut;** and **1 (12-ounce) can evaporated milk**; stir until combined. Cover with lid and cook on Low setting 4 to 5 hours or on High setting 2½ to 3 hours. To serve, stir in optional **1 tablespoon dark rum**. Let pudding stand 10 minutes prior to serving. If desired, top with **⅔ cup toasted sweetened flaked coconut**. Serves 4.

....

EACH SERVING: ABOUT 300 CALORIES, 4G PROTEIN, 47G CARBOHYDRATE, 11G TOTAL FAT (9G SATURATED), 1G FIBER, 11MG CHOLESTEROL, 65MG SODIUM.

PECAN-STUFFED "BAKED" APPLES

Trim bottom ¼-inch off **6 cored Gala apples** so they sit flat; place in 7- to 8-quart slow cooker bowl. In medium bowl, with fingers, combine **½ cup chopped pecans**; **⅔ cup dried tart cherries**; **4 tablespoons soft butter**; **¼ cup brown sugar**; **¼ teaspoon allspice**; **¼ teaspoon pepper**; and **pinch of salt**. Stuff into centers of apples. Pour **¼ cup apple juice** around apples. Cover bowl with lid and cook on Low 4 hours or until tender. Serve warm with ice cream. Serves 6.

EACH SERVING: ABOUT 285 CALORIES, 1G PROTEIN, 42G CARBOHYDRATE, 14G TOTAL FAT (5G SATURATED), 7G FIBER, 20MG CHOLESTEROL, 95MG SODIUM.

SLOW COOKER PEPPERMINT BARK HOT CHOCOLATE

A cross between a seasonal obsession and a winter cocktail: Into a 7-quart slow cooker bowl, add **8 cups whole milk**; **1 (14-ounce) can sweetened condensed milk**; **3 cups bittersweet** or **semi-sweet chocolate chips**; **¼ cup crème de menthe** or **vodka** (optional); **1 tablespoon vanilla extract**; **1 teaspoon peppermint extract**; and ¼ **teaspoon salt**. Cover and cook on High 2 hours or until combined, whisking vigorously halfway through to help chocolate melt. Switch to Warm setting for serving. Serve with dollops of whipped cream and crushed candy canes for garnish. Serves 12.

EACH SERVING: ABOUT 419 CALORIES, 12G PROTEIN, 45KG CARBOHYDRATE, 45G TOTAL FAT (15G SATURATED), 4G FIBER, 28MG CHOLESTEROL, 161MG SODIUM.

FALL FRUIT COMPOTE

In 4½- to 6-quart slow cooker bowl, toss **4 large cooking apples (like Cortland or Rome Beauty)** and **3 large, firm pears like Bosc**, all peeled and cut into 1-inch chunks; ⅓ **cup packed brown sugar**; **½ cup dried fruit such as cranberries, cherries**, or **raisins**; **1 tablespoon cornstarch**; and **¼ teaspoon ground cinnamon**. Cover slow cooker with lid and cook on Low setting 5 to 6 hours or on High setting 3 to 3½ hours. If desired, stir in 2 tablespoons trans-fat free margarine or butter when compote is done. Serve compote warm with ice cream if you like. Makes 5 cups or 8 servings.

EACH SERVING: ABOUT 165 CALORIES, 1G PROTEIN, 43G CARBOHYDRATE, 1G TOTAL FAT (0G SATURATED), 2G FIBER, 0MG CHOLESTEROL, 4MG SODIUM.

Tried & Tested
Slow Cookers

If any of these slow cooker recipes inspires an upgrade, we've got you covered.
After simmering stew in the newest models, here are the best in class.

···················· BEST BUDGET BUYS ····················

BELLA DOTS
6-QUART SLOW COOKER ($35)
Make sure you're home when dinner's ready,
since this slow cooker won't automatically
put itself into a keep-warm setting. It comes in
eight bold colors to dress up your table.
bellahousewares.com

HAMILTON BEACH STOVETOP-SAFE
PROGRAMMABLE SLOW COOKER ($80)
A nonstick insert you can heat on the stove
for browning means no extra pot to wash.
The cooker auto-flips to a keep-warm (154°F)
cycle so food won't dry out.
hamiltonbeach.com

···················· BEST OVERALL ····················

CUISINART COOK CENTRAL 3-IN-1
MULTICOOKER MSC-600 ($159)
This one lets you sear meat right in
the 6-quart cooker. When it's finished,
the appliance automatically kicks into
keep-warm mode, and it won't stay so
hot that your food overcooks.
cuisinart.com

THE 3-QUART HAMILTON BEACH OVAL SLOW COOKER 33234 ($20)
It's smaller than usual, but still big enough to hold a whole chicken or a petite roast—and lightweight, too. The one downside: It doesn't have a programmable timer. *hamiltonbeach.com*

CALPHALON 4-QUART DIGITAL SLOW COOKER ($80)
You won't feed a crowd with this crock, but it can hold a whole four-pound chicken and deliver a hearty stew for four. It's also programmable for up to 24 hours and can keep food simmering so you'll always come home to a hot meal. *calphalon.com*

································· BEST FOR VERSATILITY ·································

NINJA COOKING SYSTEM ($180)
This multitasker has settings for browning, baking, and roasting—which offers many cooking options. It serves up truly delicious fare, like a roast as good as oven-cooked and a super beef stew.
ninjakitchen.com

································· BEST FOR ENTERTAINING ·································

CROCK-POT HOOK UP CONNECTABLE ENTERTAINING SYSTEM ($140)
These connectable cookers plug into one another so you can create a buffet. Or, choose among individual units: two 1-quart oval crocks ($50), a 2-quart round one ($40) or a 3.5-quart oval one ($60). Available in green, blue, red or gray. *crock-pot.com*

Chicken Fricassee
(page 30)

1 Poultry

Slow cooker options for poultry like chicken and turkey are countless. There's minimal meat prep work involved (compared to beef or pork) and the cooking time is quick, with some recipes at just 3 to 4 hours on a high setting.

Red-Cooked Turkey Thighs with Leeks and Slow-Simmered Turkey, Pot Pie Style will both remind you that turkey isn't just for the holidays. Cost-effective pound per pound, turkey is nutrient-loaded as well. Ditch the grill and impress with the smoky Barbecue Turkey with Corn Salad or Tangy BBQ Chicken. This chapter is brimming with Italian dishes that no one would know you didn't slave over a stove for like Chicken Cacciatore and Chicken Scarpariello. Go global with the spice-rubbed Caribbean Chicken Thighs, Moroccan-style Chicken Tagine, or salsa-spiked Latin Chicken with Black Beans and Sweet Potatoes. Pick your poultry and awe your entire family with the results.

Barbecue Turkey
WITH CORN SALAD

These fall-apart-tender turkey thighs get their spicy sweetness from a dry rub of cayenne pepper, paprika, and brown sugar. The paired corn salad gets a kick from a spoonful of the homemade barbecue sauce.

ACTIVE TIME: 25 MINUTES   COOKING TIME: 6 HOURS ON LOW OR 3 HOURS ON HIGH
MAKES: 6 MAIN-DISH SERVINGS

1   teaspoon mustard powder

1   tablespoon plus 1 teaspoon sweet paprika

3   tablespoons packed dark brown sugar

3/4   teaspoon ground red pepper (cayenne)

salt and ground black pepper

4   (4 pounds) bone-in turkey thighs, skin removed

1   cup plus 2 tablespoons water

1/2   cup plus 3 tablespoons cider vinegar

1/2   cup ketchup

1   package (10 ounces) frozen lima beans

2   cups fresh corn kernels (from 3 ears of corn)

2   stalks celery, sliced

4   medium carrots, peeled and thinly sliced at an angle

1   In small bowl, combine mustard powder, 1 tablespoon paprika, 1 tablespoon brown sugar, 1/2 teaspoon ground red pepper, and 1/2 teaspoon each salt and pepper. Place turkey in large dish and rub spice mixture all over meat. Spice-rubbed turkey can be covered and refrigerated up to 1 day ahead of cooking.

2   In 6-quart slow cooker bowl, combine 1 cup water and 1/4 cup vinegar. Place turkey in slow cooker in single layer, overlapping pieces slightly if necessary. Cover and cook on Low 6 hours or on High 3 hours, or until instant-read thermometer inserted in thickest part reaches 165°F and meat is tender when pierced with tip of paring knife.

3   In 2-quart saucepan, combine ketchup, 1/4 cup vinegar, remaining 1 teaspoon paprika, 2 tablespoons brown sugar, 1/4 teaspoon cayenne, and 2 tablespoons water. Heat to boiling on medium, stirring, then reduce heat to maintain steady simmer; cook 5 minutes or until thickened, stirring occasionally. Barbecue sauce can be refrigerated in airtight container for up to 1 week.

4   Cook lima beans as label directs; drain, rinse under cold water until cool, and drain again. In large bowl, toss corn, celery, carrots, lima beans, 1 tablespoon barbecue sauce, and remaining 3 tablespoons vinegar.

5   Serve turkey thighs with barbecue sauce and corn salad.

EACH SERVING: ABOUT 430 CALORIES, 44G PROTEIN, 30G CARBOHYDRATE, 11G TOTAL FAT (3G SATURATED), 6G FIBER, 112MG CHOLESTEROL, 715MG SODIUM.

CREAMY
Chicken and Potatoes

Think all of the luscious comfort of Chicken Pot Pie without the multi-step prep. Don't be afraid to use peas in the slow cooker: just add the thawed peas right at the end, like in this recipe. Serve with biscuits if you like!

ACTIVE TIME: 20 MINUTES   COOKING TIME: 8 HOURS ON LOW OR 6 HOURS ON HIGH
MAKES: 6 MAIN-DISH SERVINGS

2   cups (½ 16-ounce bag) peeled baby carrots

1   pound red potatoes, each cut into quarters

1   small onion, coarsely chopped

1   clove garlic, crushed with press

1   (3½- to 4-pound) cut-up chicken, skin removed from all pieces except wings

1   cup chicken broth

3   tablespoons cornstarch

½   teaspoon dried thyme

salt and ground black pepper

1   package (10 ounces) frozen peas, thawed

½   cup heavy or whipping cream

1 In 5- to 6-quart slow cooker, combine carrots, potatoes, onion, and garlic. Place chicken pieces on top of vegetables. In 2-cup liquid measuring cup, with fork, mix chicken broth, cornstarch, thyme, 1 teaspoon salt, and ¼ teaspoon pepper; pour mixture over chicken and vegetables. Cover slow cooker with lid and cook, on Low 8 hours or on High 6 hours.

2 With tongs or slotted spoon, transfer chicken pieces to warm deep platter. With slotted spoon, transfer vegetables to platter with chicken pieces. Cover platter to keep warm. Stir peas and cream into cooking liquid; heat through. Spoon sauce over chicken and vegetables on platter.

EACH SERVING: ABOUT 380 CALORIES, 36G PROTEIN, 30G CARBOHYDRATE, 12G TOTAL FAT (6G SATURATED), 4G FIBER, 127MG CHOLESTEROL, 680MG SODIUM.

CLASSIC
Chicken Soup

This comforting classic subs skinless breasts and thighs for a whole fryer, so there's no fat to skim. Simmered for hours, the chicken becomes the flavor shortcut for leftover pot pie. To make, transfer $1/3$ of vegetables, 1 chicken breast, and 1 chicken thigh to container; refrigerate up to 3 days.

ACTIVE TIME: 25 MINUTES   **COOKING TIME:** 6 HOURS   **MAKES:** 6 MAIN-DISH SERVINGS

1   tablespoon vegetable oil

1   jumbo sweet onion (1 pound), finely chopped

salt and ground black pepper

1½ pounds fennel (2 large)

1   pound carrots

12 ounces Yukon Gold potatoes (2 large)

8   ounces celery stalks (4 large)

1   bay leaf

1½ pounds bone-in chicken thighs, skin removed

1½ pounds bone-in chicken breasts, skin removed

1   quart low-sodium chicken broth

1   tablespoon packed fresh dill leaves

1 In 12-inch skillet, heat oil on medium-low. Add onion and ¼ teaspoon salt. Cook 15 minutes or until golden brown and tender, stirring occasionally.

2 While onion cooks, trim and cut fennel into ¼-inch-thick slices. Cut carrots into quarters lengthwise, then into 3-inch-long pieces. Cut potatoes into ¼-inch-thick half-moons. Thinly slice celery.

3 In 6-quart slow cooker bowl, evenly spread carrots, potatoes, fennel, celery, and bay leaf. Arrange chicken pieces on top, pressing into vegetables; sprinkle with ½ teaspoon each salt and black pepper. Spread hot onion over chicken. Add broth, cover immediately with lid, and cook on Low 6 hours.

4 Stir in dill. Divide vegetables among serving bowls. Remove meat from chicken and divide among serving bowls. Stir ¼ teaspoon salt into soup. Ladle over vegetable-chicken mixture.

EACH SERVING: ABOUT 465 CALORIES, 20G PROTEIN, 44G CARBOHYDRATE, 25G TOTAL FAT (11G SATURATED), 5G FIBER, 83MG CHOLESTEROL, 690MG SODIUM.

Leftover Revamp: To make **Chicken Pot Pie**, preheat oven to 425°F. Transfer ½ **cup potatoes from reserved vegetable mixture** to large bowl. With potato masher, mash until crushed. Stir in ½ **cup heavy cream** and mash until well combined. Remove meat from **reserved chicken**, shred into large chunks, and add to potato mixture. Add **reserved vegetables, 1 cup frozen peas**, thawed; ½ **teaspoon freshly grated lemon peel**; ¼ **teaspoon salt**; and ¼ **teaspoon ground black pepper**. Stir until well mixed. Spread mixture, in even layer, into 9½-inch (2½-quart) deep-dish pie plate. Center **1 refrigerated piecrust** (from 14-ounce package) on top. Fold dough overhand under to make edge flush with rim of pie plate. Gently press edge against pie plate. Cut 5 slits on top. Bake 25 minutes. Cover rim of dough with foil, then bake 5 to 10 minutes longer or until crust is golden brown on top. Serves 4.

EACH SERVING: ABOUT 465 CALORIES, 20G PROTEIN, 44G CARBOHYDRATE, 25G TOTAL FAT (11G SATURATED), 5G FIBER, 83MG CHOLESTEROL, 690MG SODIUM.

TEX-MEX
Chicken Soup

Classic chicken soup gets a makeover inspired by spicy Southwestern cuisine. Note that 2 teaspoons of lemon juice can sub for the lime juice.

ACTIVE TIME: 15 MINUTES   **COOKING TIME:** 4 HOURS   **MAKES:** 6 MAIN-DISH SERVINGS

2 medium russet potatoes, peeled and cut into ½-inch chunks

¼ cup water

1 pound skinless, boneless chicken breast halves, cut into quarters

1 pound skinless, boneless chicken thighs, cut into halves

4 cups chicken broth

3 large celery stalks, thinly sliced

1 jalapeño chile, finely chopped

2 teaspoons ground cumin

1 clove garlic, crushed with press

salt and ground black pepper

2 cups frozen corn, thawed

½ cup lightly packed fresh cilantro leaves, finely chopped

1 tablespoon lime juice

1 ripe avocado, peeled and chopped

1 In large microwavable bowl, combine potatoes and water. Cover with vented plastic wrap and microwave on high 5 minutes or until almost tender. Drain and transfer potatoes to bowl of 7- to 8-quart slow cooker.

2 To same slow cooker bowl, add chicken, broth, celery, jalapeño, cumin, garlic, 1 teaspoon salt, and ¼ teaspoon pepper. Cover with lid and cook on Low 4 hours or until chicken is cooked through (165°F) but not soft.

3 Transfer chicken to cutting board. Using two forks, pull chicken into bite-size pieces. Return chicken to slow cooker bowl. Stir corn, cilantro, and lime juice into soup. Divide among serving bowls. Top with avocado.

EACH SERVING: ABOUT 340 CALORIES, 35G PROTEIN, 25G CARBOHYDRATE, 11G TOTAL FAT (2G SATURATED), 5G FIBER, 124MG CHOLESTEROL, 1,215MG SODIUM.

MOROCCAN-SPICED
Chicken

Dark meat delivers major flavor for pennies—it's usually priced at about $2 per pound. Pumpkin-pie spice is a blend of cinnamon, ginger, nutmeg, allspice, and cloves that is a shortcut for warm spices in one scoop.

ACTIVE TIME: 25 MINUTES   **COOKING TIME:** 5 HOURS, PLUS MARINATING
MAKES: 6 MAIN-DISH SERVINGS

2½ pounds bone-in skinless chicken thighs

1   teaspoon ground cumin

½   teaspoon ground coriander

½   teaspoon pumpkin-pie spice

salt and ground black pepper

1½ cups chicken broth

1   can (15 ounces) diced fire-roasted tomatoes, drained

1   can (15 ounces) white kidney (cannellini) beans, rinsed and drained

1   large sweet potato, peeled and chopped

1   medium onion (6 to 8 ounces), chopped

½   cup dried apricots, sliced

cooked couscous, for serving

sliced almonds, to garnish

1 In a gallon-size resealable plastic bag, combine chicken thighs with cumin, coriander, pumpkin-pie spice, and ½ teaspoon each salt and pepper; refrigerate overnight.

2 In 6- to 7-quart slow cooker bowl, combine chicken broth, tomatoes, beans, sweet potato, onion, and apricots. Place chicken in slow cooker bowl on top of vegetables.

3 Cover and cook 5 hours on Low or until chicken is cooked through (165°F). Transfer chicken to cutting board. Skim and discard fat from cooking liquid. Stir ¼ teaspoon salt into cooking liquid.

4 Serve chicken and vegetables over cooked couscous. Drizzle with cooking liquid and garnish with sliced almonds.

EACH SERVING: ABOUT 340 CALORIES, 31G PROTEIN, 28G CARBOHYDRATE, 11G TOTAL FAT (3G SATURATED), 5G FIBER, 97MG CHOLESTEROL, 750MG SODIUM.

RED-COOKED
Turkey Thighs
WITH LEEKS

This Chinese-inspired dish features succulent meat simmered in a soy and fresh ginger sauce. Skip any additional salt on this one—the soy sauce does it all.

ACTIVE TIME: 20 MINUTES   **COOKING TIME:** 10 HOURS ON LOW OR 5 HOURS ON HIGH
MAKES: 6 MAIN-DISH SERVINGS

- 4   large leeks
- ½   cup dry sherry
- ⅓   cup soy sauce
- ¼   cup packed brown sugar
- 2   tablespoons peeled, minced fresh ginger
- 1   teaspoon Chinese five-spice powder
- 3   small (about 1 pound each) turkey thighs, bone-in, skin removed
- 3   cloves garlic, crushed with press
- 2   cups (about half a 16-ounce bag) peeled baby carrots

1   Cut off root and dark-green tops from leeks. Discard tough outer leaves. Cut each leek lengthwise in half then crosswise in half. Rinse leeks in large bowl of cold water, swishing to remove sand. Transfer leeks to colander, leaving sand in bowl. Repeat several times, until no sand remains. Drain well.

2   In 4½- to 6-quart slow cooker bowl, combine sherry, soy sauce, sugar, ginger, and five-spice powder. Add leeks, turkey, garlic, and carrots, and toss to coat with soy mixture. Cover slow cooker with lid and cook on Low setting 8 to 10 hours or on High setting 4 to 5 hours.

3   Transfer turkey and vegetables to deep platter. Skim and discard fat from cooking liquid. Spoon cooking liquid over turkey and vegetables.

EACH SERVING: ABOUT 355 CALORIES, 41G PROTEIN, 24G CARBOHYDRATE, 10G TOTAL FAT (3G SATURATED), 2G FIBER, 112MG CHOLESTEROL, 1,005MG SODIUM.

CHICKEN **Cacciatore**

Slow cooking this classic dish creates tender chicken that's infused with bold flavor. Pickled cherry peppers give it kick. Other ways to add the oomph: Swap in ¼ cup drained pepperoncini or ½ teaspoon crushed red pepper.

ACTIVE TIME: 15 MINUTES   **COOKING TIME:** 5 HOURS   **MAKES:** 4 MAIN-DISH SERVINGS

1   cup chicken broth

1   can (6 ounces) tomato paste

2½ pounds bone-in chicken thighs, skin removed

salt and ground black pepper

2   medium red peppers, seeded and sliced

12 ounces cremini (baby bella) mushrooms, trimmed and cut into halves or quarters, if large

1   medium onion (6 to 8 ounces), chopped

2   pickled cherry peppers, chopped

2   cloves garlic, crushed with press

2   small sprigs fresh rosemary

cooked polenta, for serving

2   tablespoons capers, drained and finely chopped, to garnish

1 In bowl of 7- to 8-quart slow cooker, whisk together broth and tomato paste.

2 Sprinkle chicken with ½ teaspoon each salt and black pepper; transfer to slow cooker bowl along with red peppers, mushrooms, onion, cherry peppers, garlic, and rosemary.

3 Cover with lid and cook on Low 5 hours or until chicken is cooked through (165°F). To serve, spoon over polenta. Garnish with capers.

....

EACH SERVING: ABOUT 300 CALORIES, 38G PROTEIN, 20G CARBOHYDRATE, 8G TOTAL FAT (2G SATURATED), 4G FIBER, 163MG CHOLESTEROL, 990MG SODIUM.

CHICKEN **Scarpariello**

This Italian-American dish was originally made with roasted or pan-fried chicken and sausage. We've added balsamic vinegar, mushrooms, and grape tomatoes to create a hearty weeknight dinner.

ACTIVE TIME: 20 MINUTES   **COOKING TIME:** 8 HOURS ON LOW OR 4 HOURS ON HIGH
MAKES: 6 MAIN-DISH SERVINGS

½ pound hot or sweet Italian sausage links, cut into 1½-inch pieces

1 medium onion (6 to 8 ounces), chopped

2 cloves garlic, crushed with press

2 tablespoons tomato paste

2 tablespoons balsamic vinegar

1 teaspoon dried Italian seasoning or dried thyme

1 pint grape tomatoes

1 package (8 ounces) cremini mushrooms, sliced

1 (3½- to 4-pound) cut-up chicken, skin removed from all pieces except wings

salt and ground black pepper

1 In 12-inch nonstick skillet, cook sausage pieces about 6 minutes over medium heat until well browned, turning occasionally. With tongs or slotted spoon, transfer sausages to 5- to 6-quart slow cooker. Add onion to skillet and cook 4 minutes or until slightly softened. Stir in garlic and cook 1 minute, stirring. Remove skillet from heat; stir in tomato paste, vinegar, and Italian seasoning until blended, then add tomatoes and mushrooms. Spoon vegetable mixture into slow cooker and stir to combine.

2 Sprinkle chicken with ¼ teaspoon salt and ¼ teaspoon pepper. In same skillet, cook chicken pieces (in 2 batches, if necessary) over medium-high heat until well browned, about 10 minutes. Place chicken on top of vegetable mixture in slow cooker. Cover slow cooker with lid and cook on Low 8 hours or on High 4 hours. Skim fat from juices before serving.

EACH SERVING: ABOUT 355 CALORIES, 39G PROTEIN, 20G CARBOHYDRATE, 8G TOTAL FAT (2G SATURATED), 4G FIBER, 163MG CHOLESTEROL, 990MG SODIUM.

TIP
No capers on hand? Replace them with ¼ cup chopped green or black olives.

CHICKEN **Fricassee**

This slow-cooked chicken dinner with mushrooms, peas, and potatoes is perfect for an at-home dinner date. A dash of lemon zest adds a citrusy brightness. For photo, see page 14.

ACTIVE TIME: 25 MINUTES   **COOKING TIME:** 5 HOURS, PLUS MARINATING   **MAKES:** 6 MAIN-DISH SERVINGS

2½ pounds bone-in skinless chicken thighs

½ teaspoon grated lemon peel

¼ teaspoon dried thyme

salt and ground black pepper

¾ cup chicken broth

1   teaspoon chicken broth base or demi-glace

1½ pounds (small) red potatoes, scrubbed and cut in half

8   ounces white mushrooms, cut in half

1   large shallot, chopped

2   cloves garlic, chopped

½ cup whole milk

1   tablespoon butter, melted

1½ cups frozen peas, thawed

⅓ cup light sour cream

chopped parsley, for garnish

1 In gallon-size resealable plastic bag, combine bone-in skinless chicken thighs with lemon peel, thyme, and ½ teaspoon each salt and pepper; refrigerate overnight.

2 In 6- to 7-quart slow cooker bowl, combine chicken broth, base/demi-glace, potatoes, mushrooms, shallot, and garlic. Place chicken in slow cooker bowl on top of vegetables. Cover and cook 5 hours on Low or until chicken is cooked through (165°F).

3 Transfer chicken to cutting board. Skim and discard fat from cooking liquid. Stir ¼ teaspoon salt into cooking liquid. Transfer potatoes to large bowl; mash with milk, melted butter, and ¼ teaspoon salt. Return chicken to slow cooker; stir in peas and sour cream. Serve over potatoes; garnish with chopped parsley.

EACH SERVING: ABOUT 380 CALORIES, 33G PROTEIN, 28G CARBOHYDRATE, 15G TOTAL FAT (6G SATURATED), 15G FIBER, 110MG CHOLESTEROL, 600MG SODIUM.

Slow-Simmered Turkey,
POT PIE STYLE

Set it and forget it! All the flavors of a pot pie without the laborious crust.

ACTIVE TIME: 15 MINUTES   **COOKING TIME:** 8 HOURS   **MAKES:** 6 MAIN-DISH SERVINGS

3   tablespoons trans-fat free margarine or butter

1   (about 2½-pound) turkey thigh, bone-in, skin removed

salt and ground black pepper

1   small onion, cut into 1-inch pieces

10 sprigs thyme

3   stalks (large) celery, each cut into 1½-inch pieces

2   cups (about ½ a 16-ounce bag) peeled baby carrots

1   pound medium red potatoes, each cut into 4 wedges

⅓   cup all-purpose flour

1   can (14 to 14½ ounces) chicken broth

¼   cup heavy or whipping cream

1   In nonstick 10-inch skillet, melt 1 tablespoon margarine or butter over medium-high heat. Add turkey to skillet; sprinkle with 1 teaspoon salt and ½ teaspoon pepper. Scatter onion around turkey. Cook turkey and onion 6 to 7 minutes or until turkey is browned on both sides.

2   Meanwhile, in 4½- to 6-quart slow cooker pot, place thyme, celery, carrots, and potatoes. Transfer turkey and onion to slow cooker.

3   Melt remaining 2 tablespoons margarine or butter in same skillet over medium heat. Add flour and cook 1 minute, stirring. Add broth and cream; heat to boiling, stirring constantly. Pour broth mixture into slow cooker. Cover slow cooker with lid and cook on Low setting, 7 to 8 hours or until turkey and vegetables are very tender.

4   To serve, discard thyme sprigs. With tongs, transfer turkey to cutting board. Cut meat from bone into bite-size pieces; return meat to slow cooker. Cover slow cooker and heat through on High setting if necessary.

EACH SERVING: ABOUT 355 CALORIES, 26G PROTEIN, 26G CARBOHYDRATE, 16G TOTAL FAT (5G SATURATED), 3G FIBER, 84MG CHOLESTEROL, 880MG SODIUM.

TANGY **BBQ Chicken**

If you prefer a thicker barbecue sauce for the chicken, boil the slow-cooked sauce in a saucepan until thickened. To use leftovers for Salad with Chicken, Apples, and Cheddar, transfer 2 chicken breasts to container; refrigerate up to 3 days.

ACTIVE TIME: 15 MINUTES   **COOKING TIME:** 4 HOURS   **MAKES:** 6 MAIN-DISH SERVINGS

1   cup ketchup

2   tablespoons spicy brown mustard

2   tablespoons balsamic vinegar

2   teaspoons Worcestershire sauce

1   clove garlic, pressed

1/4   teaspoon smoked paprika

salt and ground black pepper

4   (3 to 3½ pounds) bone-in chicken breast halves, skin removed

4   (1½ pounds) chicken drumsticks, skin removed

coleslaw, for serving

1   Spray 6-quart slow cooker bowl with nonstick cooking spray.

2   In medium bowl, with wire whisk, stir together ketchup, mustard, vinegar, Worcestershire sauce, garlic, smoked paprika, and ⅛ teaspoon ground black pepper; transfer half of sauce to slow cooker bowl.

3   Sprinkle chicken with ½ teaspoon salt and ¼ teaspoon ground black pepper; add to slow cooker bowl. Spoon remaining sauce over and around chicken to coat. Cover with lid and cook on High 4 hours, or until chicken is no longer pink.

4   Transfer chicken to serving platter. Whisk cooking liquid until well mixed; drizzle over chicken. Serve chicken with coleslaw and any remaining sauce.

EACH SERVING: ABOUT 320 CALORIES, 44G PROTEIN, 18G CARBOHYDRATE, 7G TOTAL FAT (2G SATURATED), 0G FIBER, 144MG CHOLESTEROL, 1,275MG SODIUM.

Leftover Revamp: To make **Salad with Chicken, Apples, and Cheddar**, remove and discard bones from reserved **2 chicken breasts**; shred meat. In large bowl, whisk **3 tablespoons olive oil, 2 tablespoons cider vinegar, 2 teaspoons Dijon mustard**, and **1/4 teaspoon** each **salt** and **pepper**. Add to same bowl: **1 head red leaf lettuce**, chopped, and **1 small red pepper**, very thinly sliced; toss until well combined. Divide among 4 serving plates; top with **1 Granny Smith apple**, thinly sliced; **chicken; 1/4 cup walnuts**, toasted and chopped; and **2 ounces extra-sharp Cheddar cheese**, coarsely grated. Serves 4.

EACH SERVING: ABOUT 400 CALORIES, 36G PROTEIN, 12G CARBOHYDRATE, 23G TOTAL FAT (6G SATURATED), 3G FIBER, 95MG CHOLESTEROL, 415MG SODIUM.

Chicken Tagine

This Moroccan stew features tender chicken and butternut squash paired with garlic, onion, and rich spices in the gentle heat of the slow cooker. Forty percent of the fat in chicken comes from the skin— so we got rid of it!

ACTIVE TIME: 20 MINUTES   **COOKING TIME:** 8 HOURS ON LOW OR 4 HOURS ON HIGH
MAKES: 6 MAIN-DISH SERVINGS

1   medium (1½-pound) butternut squash, peeled and cut into 2-inch chunks

2   medium tomatoes, coarsely chopped

1   medium onion (6 to 8 ounces), chopped

2   cloves garlic, crushed with press

1   can (15 to 19 ounces) garbanzo beans, rinsed and drained

1   cup chicken broth

⅓   cup raisins

2   teaspoons ground coriander

2   teaspoons ground cumin

½   teaspoon ground cinnamon

salt and ground black pepper

3   pounds bone-in skinless chicken thighs

1   box (10 ounces) plain couscous

½   cup pitted green olives

1 In 6-quart slow cooker, combine squash, tomatoes, onion, garlic, beans, broth, and raisins. In cup, combine coriander, cumin, cinnamon, ½ teaspoon salt, and ¼ teaspoon pepper. Rub spice mixture all over chicken thighs; place chicken on top of vegetable mixture. Cover slow cooker with lid and cook, on Low 8 hours or on High 4 hours.

2 About 10 minutes before serving, prepare couscous as label directs.

3 To serve, fluff couscous with fork. Stir olives into chicken mixture. Serve chicken mixture over couscous.

EACH SERVING: ABOUT 545 CALORIES, 39G PROTEIN, 80G CARBOHYDRATE, 9G TOTAL FAT (2G SATURATED), 10G FIBER, 107MG CHOLESTEROL, 855MG SODIUM.

TIP
To peel butternut squash, lay it on its side. Using a sharp knife, cut into 2-inch rounds. Place rounds flat-side down and cut away the peel. Scoop out seeds and cut as desired.

CARIBBEAN
Chicken Thighs

Going low and slow is the key to creating amazing texture and layers of flavor. A tropical fruit salsa of mango and avocado chunks for topping continues the island-love. Serve with a side of black beans.

ACTIVE TIME: 15 MINUTES   **COOKING TIME:** 8 HOURS ON LOW OR 4 HOURS ON HIGH
MAKES: 4 MAIN-DISH SERVINGS

2   pounds (about 2 large) sweet potatoes, peeled and sliced into ½-inch-thick rounds

¼   cup no-pulp orange juice

¼   cup chicken broth

salt

5   cloves garlic

1   jalapeño chile, chopped

2   tablespoons olive oil

2   tablespoons cumin

1   teaspoon dried thyme

3   pounds bone-in skinless chicken thighs

1   mango, peeled and cubed

1   avocado, peeled and cubed

1   tablespoon fresh lime juice (from about 2 limes)

1 In 6- or 7-quart slow cooker bowl, layer sweet potato slices. In a small bowl, mix orange juice, chicken broth, and ¼ teaspoon salt; pour over potatoes.

2 In a food processor, blend garlic, jalapeño, olive oil, cumin, and thyme into smooth paste. Sprinkle chicken thighs with ¼ teaspoon salt. Arrange chicken over sweet potatoes and then spread with garlic mixture. Cover slow cooker with lid and cook, on Low 8 hours or on High 4 hours.

3 About 5 minutes before serving, in a small bowl, toss mango, avocado, lime juice, and pinch of salt. Top chicken with salsa and serve with sweet potatoes.

....

EACH SERVING: ABOUT 595 CALORIES, 44G PROTEIN, 53G CARBOHYDRATE, 24G TOTAL FAT (4G SATURATED), 10G FIBER, 192MG CHOLESTEROL, 625MG SODIUM.

CAJUN SURF 'N' TURF
Stew

Use your slow cooker to create a gumbo-style stew loaded with chicken, shrimp, and andouille sausage. Supermarket out of andouille? The smoked Polish sausage, kielbasa, delivers a similar flavor.

ACTIVE TIME: 30 MINUTES   **COOKING TIME:** 6 HOURS ON LOW OR 4 HOURS ON HIGH
MAKES: 8 MAIN-DISH SERVINGS

¼ cup vegetable oil

¼ cup all-purpose flour

2 medium green peppers, chopped

1 large red pepper, chopped

3 medium celery stalks, sliced

1 large onion (12 ounces), chopped

salt and ground black pepper

2 pounds skinless, boneless chicken thighs, cut into 1-inch chunks

12 ounces fresh or frozen okra

6 ounces andouille sausage, sliced

1½ cups chicken broth

½ teaspoon ground red pepper (cayenne)

¼ teaspoon dried thyme

12 ounces (16- to 20-count) shrimp, shelled and deveined

cooked white rice, for serving

1 In 6-quart saucepot, heat oil on medium. Sprinkle in flour, whisking to combine. Reduce heat to medium-low. Cook 10 to 15 minutes or until brown, whisking constantly.

2 To same pot, add peppers, celery, onion, and ¼ teaspoon salt. Increase heat to medium. Cook 4 minutes, stirring. Transfer to 7- to 8-quart slow cooker bowl; stir in chicken, okra, sausage, broth, ground red pepper, thyme, 1 teaspoon salt, and ½ teaspoon black pepper. Cover with lid and cook on Low 6 hours or High 4 hours or until chicken is cooked through (165°F).

3 Once chicken is cooked, add shrimp to slow cooker bowl. If cooking on Low, increase heat to High. Cook, covered, another 5 minutes or until shrimp are cooked through. Serve with rice.

EACH SERVING: ABOUT 325 CALORIES, 34G PROTEIN, 13G CARBOHYDRATE, 16G TOTAL FAT (3G SATURATED), 3G FIBER, 175MG CHOLESTEROL, 1,065MG SODIUM.

NORTH AFRICAN
Chicken Stew
WITH DRIED PLUMS

Dried plums don't just lend fruity sweetness to this luscious dish;
they are also a fiber powerhouse that can promote bone health
and help maintain blood sugar levels.

ACTIVE TIME: 15 MINUTES   **COOKING TIME:** 8 HOURS   **MAKES:** 6 MAIN-DISH SERVINGS

1   tablespoon ground coriander

1   tablespoon ground cumin

salt

1/2   teaspoon ground cinnamon

2   pounds (about 6 large) skinless, bone-in chicken thighs

1   tablespoon vegetable oil

2   cups (about 1/2 a 16-ounce bag) peeled baby carrots

1/2   cup whole pitted dried plums (prunes)

1   can (15 to 19 ounces) garbanzo beans, rinsed and drained

1   cup chicken broth

1   box (10 ounces) plain couscous

2   plum tomatoes, coarsely chopped

1   box (9 ounces) frozen whole green beans, thawed

1 In small bowl, combine coriander, cumin, 3/4 teaspoon salt, and cinnamon; use to rub all over chicken.

2 In nonstick 12-inch skillet, heat oil over medium-high heat until hot; add chicken and cook 7 to 8 minutes or until browned on both sides. Meanwhile, in 4 1/2- to 6-quart slow cooker pot, place carrots, dried plums, and garbanzo beans.

3 Add browned chicken to slow cooker. Remove skillet from heat. Add broth to skillet and stir until browned bits are loosened from bottom. Pour broth mixture into slow cooker.

4 Cover slow cooker with lid and cook on Low 7 to 8 hours or until chicken and carrots are tender.

5 About 10 minutes before serving, prepare couscous as label directs. Stir tomatoes and green beans into stew. Cover slow cooker and heat through on High setting if necessary. To serve, fluff couscous with fork. Spoon into bowls; top with chicken and sauce.

EACH SERVING: ABOUT 530 CALORIES, 34G PROTEIN, 75G CARBOHYDRATE, 9G TOTAL FAT (2G SATURATED), 90MG CHOLESTEROL, 740MG SODIUM.

TARRAGON **Chicken**

French flavor meets American ingenuity in this low and slow riff on a classic.

ACTIVE TIME: 15 MINUTES   **COOKING TIME:** 10 HOURS ON LOW OR 5 HOURS ON HIGH
MAKES: 4 MAIN-DISH SERVINGS

2   cups (about half a 16-ounce bag) peeled baby carrots

1   package (8 ounces) mushrooms, each cut into quarters

1   small onion, chopped

8   (about 2½ pounds) small bone-in skinless chicken thighs

1   cup chicken broth

3   tablespoons cornstarch

1   teaspoon dried tarragon or 2 tablespoons chopped fresh tarragon leaves

salt and ground black pepper

½   cup heavy or whipping cream

1   In 4½- to 6-quart slow cooker bowl, combine carrots, mushrooms, and onion. Place chicken on top of vegetables. In 2-cup liquid measuring cup, with fork, mix broth, cornstarch, tarragon, 1 teaspoon salt, and ½ teaspoon pepper; pour mixture over chicken and vegetables. Cover slow cooker with lid and cook as manufacturer directs on Low setting 8 to 10 hours or on High setting 4 to 5 hours.

2   With slotted spoon, transfer chicken and vegetables to warm deep platter. Skim and discard fat from cooking liquid. Stir in cream; heat through if necessary. Spoon sauce over chicken and vegetables.

EACH SERVING: ABOUT 370 CALORIES, 35G PROTEIN, 16G CARBOHYDRATE, 18G TOTAL FAT (9G SATURATED), 2G FIBER, 175MG CHOLESTEROL, 975MG SODIUM.

Latin Chicken
WITH BLACK BEANS AND SWEET POTATOES

Thanks to black beans and sweet potatoes, this spicy, smoky dish boasts a good portion of your daily fiber and beta carotene. And with just 15 minutes of prep, this slow-cooker meal is a cinch to throw together in the morning.

ACTIVE TIME: 15 MINUTES   **COOKING TIME:** 8 HOURS ON LOW OR 4 HOURS ON HIGH
MAKES: 6 MAIN-DISH SERVINGS

3   pounds bone-in skinless chicken thighs

2   teaspoons ground cumin

salt and ground black pepper

1   teaspoon smoked paprika or ½ teaspoon chopped chipotle chiles in adobo sauce

½   teaspoon ground allspice

1   cup chicken broth

½   cup salsa

3   cloves (large) garlic, crushed with press

2   cans (15 to 19 ounces each) black beans, rinsed and drained

2   pounds sweet potatoes, peeled and cut into 2-inch chunks

1   jarred roasted red pepper, cut into strips (1 cup)

⅓   cup loosely packed fresh cilantro leaves, chopped

lime wedges, for serving

1 Sprinkle chicken thighs with ½ teaspoon ground cumin, ¼ teaspoon salt, and ¼ teaspoon pepper. Heat 12-inch nonstick skillet over medium-high heat until hot; add chicken thighs and cook until well browned on all sides, about 10 minutes. Transfer chicken to plate. Remove skillet from heat.

2 In same skillet, combine smoked paprika or chipotle chiles, allspice, chicken broth, salsa, garlic, and remaining 1½ teaspoons cumin.

3 In 6-quart slow cooker, combine beans and sweet potatoes. Place chicken on top of potato mixture in slow cooker; pour broth mixture over chicken. Cover slow cooker with lid and cook, on Low 8 hours or on High 4 hours.

4 With tongs or slotted spoon, remove chicken pieces to large platter. Gently stir roasted red pepper strips into potato mixture. Spoon mixture over chicken. Sprinkle with cilantro and serve with lime wedges.

EACH SERVING: ABOUT 415 CALORIES, 36G PROTEIN, 61G CARBOHYDRATE, 6G TOTAL FAT (1G SATURATED), 12G FIBER, 107MG CHOLESTEROL, 875MG SODIUM.

Pot Roast with Red Wine Sauce
(page 56)

2 | Beef

For the most succulent, melt-in-your-mouth beef, cooking slow and low is the preferred method. Traditional recipes for Ropa Vieja call for the flank steaks to be stewed low and slow to get the sought-after shredding quality—the slow cooker is made for this!

Beef short ribs become meltingly soft in Ginger and Soy-Braised Short Ribs while brown ale provides robustness to boneless beef chuck in Beer-Braised Beef Stew. Or dial up the comfort factor with a choice of two types of chili: the chipotle-enhanced Smoky Beef Party Chili or the Chunky Chili with Beans. Take the stress out of entertaining with Provençal Stew served with crusty bread or Pot Roast with Red Wine Sauce.

CUBAN-STYLE **Beef**

Serve this tangy pulled beef with a side of saffron-spiked yellow Spanish rice.

ACTIVE TIME: 30 MINUTES   **COOKING TIME:** 10 HOURS   **MAKES:** 12 MAIN-DISH SERVINGS

1   (4-pound) boneless beef chuck roast, tied

1   teaspoon dried oregano

1   teaspoon ground cumin

salt and ground black pepper

2   teaspoons vegetable oil

1   large onion (12 ounces), sliced

1   large green pepper, sliced

1   large red pepper, sliced

2   cloves garlic, minced

2   tablespoons water

1   can (28 ounces) crushed tomatoes

½   cup pimento-stuffed green olives, sliced

chopped parsley, for garnish

Spanish rice, for serving (optional)

1 Rub beef chuck roast with oregano, cumin, and ½ teaspoon each salt and pepper. In 12-inch skillet, heat vegetable oil on medium-high until very hot. Brown roast on all sides. Transfer to 6- to 7-quart slow cooker bowl.

2 To skillet, add onion, peppers, garlic, water, and ¼ teaspoon salt; cook on medium-high 2 to 4 minutes or until slightly softened, stirring. Add crushed tomatoes. Simmer 4 minutes, stirring. Transfer vegetables and liquids to slow cooker bowl. Cover; cook 10 hours on Low or until tender.

3 Shred meat (discarding fat and gristle). With slotted spoon, transfer vegetables to large serving bowl. Stir in meat, pimento-stuffed green olives, and ¼ teaspoon salt. Serve with yellow Spanish rice. Garnish with parsley, if desired.

EACH SERVING: ABOUT 245 CALORIES, 33G PROTEIN, 9G CARBOHYDRATE, 8G TOTAL FAT (3G SATURATED), 2G FIBER, 96MG CHOLESTEROL, 435MG SODIUM.

PULLED BARBECUE **Beef**

Kick-up midweek dinners with this smoky-sweet sauce. A quick sear on the short ribs before their slow cooking stint adds more prep time, but develops a rich flavor that makes it worth it.

ACTIVE TIME: 20 MINUTES   **COOKING TIME:** 10 HOURS ON LOW OR 5 HOURS ON HIGH
MAKES: 6 MAIN-DISH SERVINGS

4   pounds bone-in beef short ribs

salt and ground black pepper

2   teaspoons vegetable oil

1   cup ketchup

2   tablespoons spicy brown mustard

1   tablespoon Worcestershire sauce

3   tablespoons red wine vinegar

1   teaspoon smoked paprika

3/4   teaspoon crushed red pepper

1/4   teaspoon onion powder

3   cups slaw mix

hamburger buns, for serving

1 Sprinkle short ribs with 1/2 teaspoon each salt and pepper. In 12-inch skillet, heat vegetable oil on medium-high until very hot. In batches, brown short ribs just on meaty sides.

2 Meanwhile, in 6- to 7-quart slow cooker bowl, whisk together ketchup, mustard, Worcestershire sauce, 1 tablespoon red wine vinegar, smoked paprika, 1/4 teaspoon crushed red pepper, and onion powder. Transfer meat to slow cooker bowl. Cover and cook 10 hours on Low or 5 hours on High, or until very tender.

3 Transfer meat to cutting board. Skim and discard fat from cooking liquid. Transfer cooking liquid to 4-quart saucepot; heat to boiling on medium-high. Boil 5 to 10 minutes or until reduced by about half. With hands, shred meat, discarding fat, bones, and gristle. Transfer meat to pot with reduced sauce; toss until well coated.

4 In large bowl, toss slaw mix with 2 tablespoons red wine vinegar, 1/2 teaspoon crushed red pepper, and 1/8 teaspoon salt. Serve meat on hamburger buns with slaw.

EACH SERVING: ABOUT 400 CALORIES, 29G PROTEIN, 31G CARBOHYDRATE, 16G TOTAL FAT (7G SATURATED), 2G FIBER, 74MG CHOLESTEROL, 835MG SODIUM.

PHILLY-STYLE BEEF
Sandwiches

Strain and discard the fat from the cooking liquid and use the broth for dipping á la a French dip sandwich.

ACTIVE TIME: 10 MINUTES   COOKING TIME: 8 HOURS   MAKES: 8 MAIN-DISH SERVINGS

1 (about 3- to 4-pound) beef chuck roast, cut into quarters

salt and ground black pepper

1 cup beef broth

3 large peppers, seeded and each cut into 6 wedges

2 medium onions (6 to 8 ounces each), peeled and each cut into 6 wedges

8 long sandwich rolls, split

16 thin slices (about 8 ounces total) Provolone or American cheese

½ cup pickled jalapeño slices, drained and chopped

1 Rub beef with 1 teaspoon salt and ½ teaspoon black pepper; add to bowl of 7- to 8-quart slow cooker along with broth. Scatter peppers and onions over beef. Cover with lid; cook on Low 8 hours or until beef is very tender.

2 When ready to serve, arrange oven rack 5 to 6 inches from broiler heat source. Preheat broiler on high.

3 Transfer beef to large cutting board. When cool enough to handle, shred meat, removing and discarding fat. Strain vegetables from cooking liquid. Reheating first, if necessary, divide meat and vegetables among rolls. Top with cheese and pickled jalapeño slices. Place sandwiches on large foil-lined jelly-roll pan and broil 2 to 3 minutes or until cheese melts.

EACH SERVING: ABOUT 580 CALORIES, 55G PROTEIN, 40G CARBOHYDRATE, 21G TOTAL FAT (10G SATURATED), 4G FIBER, 140MG CHOLESTEROL, 915MG SODIUM.

SMOKY BEEF PARTY
Chili

This designed-for-a-crowd dish keeps costs down by upping the bean to meat ratio. If you don't have two slow cookers, half (or all) of the chili can be made a day ahead and refrigerated. To reheat, transfer to Dutch oven and heat on medium until chili comes to a simmer; reduce heat to low, cover, and simmer 30 minutes to heat through.

ACTIVE TIME: 35 MINUTES **COOKING TIME:** ABOUT 6 HOURS **MAKES:** ABOUT 20 MAIN-DISH SERVINGS

- 4 cans (15 to 19 ounces) beans, preferably an assortment of pinto, black, and red beans
- 1 can (7 ounces) chipotle chiles in adobo
- 2 cans (28 ounces each) diced fire-roasted tomatoes
- 2 large onions (10 to 12 ounces each), finely chopped
- 2 medium green peppers (6 to 8 ounces each), finely chopped
- 4 cloves garlic, crushed with press
- 5 pounds beef chuck, cut into 1-inch chunks
- 2 tablespoons ground cumin
- 1 tablespoon dried oregano

salt and ground black pepper

- 1 cup shredded Monterey Jack cheese
- 1 cup reduced-fat sour cream
- 1 cup packed fresh cilantro leaves, coarsely chopped
- 2 limes, cut into wedges

1 In large colander, drain beans. Rinse well and drain again. Remove 2 chiles from can of chipotle chiles in adobo and finely chop. Place in large bowl with 2 teaspoons adobo. Reserve another 4 teaspoons adobo for cooked chili, and save remaining chiles and adobo for another use.

2 To large bowl with chiles and adobo, add tomatoes, onions, peppers, and garlic; mix well. In another large bowl, combine beef, cumin, oregano, ¼ teaspoon salt, and ¼ teaspoon pepper.

3 In each of two 7-quart slow cooker bowls, spread a generous layer of tomato mixture. Divide beef, then beans, between slow cooker bowls and top with remaining tomato mixture. Cover slow cookers with lids and cook on High setting 6 hours.

4 Using slotted spoon, transfer solids to large serving bowl. Transfer cooking liquid from slow cooker bowls to 8-cup liquid measuring cup. Remove and discard fat. Pour off and discard all but 4 cups cooking liquid. Stir reserved adobo into cooking liquid; pour over chili in bowl and stir to combine. Serve with Monterey Jack, sour cream, cilantro, and limes on the side.

EACH SERVING: ABOUT 325 CALORIES, 32G PROTEIN, 23G CARBOHYDRATE, 12G TOTAL FAT (5G SATURATED), 7G FIBER, 71MG CHOLESTEROL, 515MG SODIUM.

SWEET AND TANGY BRAISED
Chuck Roast

Less tender cuts of meat like a chuck roast aren't just lower in cost, they are especially well-suited for slow cooking. This classic piece of beef is given a sweet treatment with gingersnap cookie crumbs and raisins.

ACTIVE TIME: 10 MINUTES   **COOKING TIME:** 10 HOURS ON LOW OR 6 HOURS ON HIGH
MAKES: 6 MAIN-DISH SERVINGS

6 (2-inch) gingersnap cookies, finely crushed into crumbs

2 cups (about ½ a 16-ounce bag) peeled baby carrots

2 large stalks celery, cut crosswise into 2-inch pieces

1 medium onion (6 to 8 ounces), cut into 1-inch pieces

1 cup dry red wine

2 tablespoons red wine vinegar

¼ cup raisins

salt and ground black pepper

1 (about 2 pounds) boneless beef chuck roast

1 In 4 ½- to 6-quart slow cooker bowl, combine gingersnap crumbs, carrots, celery, onion, wine, vinegar, raisins, 1 teaspoon salt, and ½ teaspoon pepper. Place roast on top of vegetables. Cover slow cooker with lid and cook on Low 8 to 10 hours or on High 6 to 6½ hours, or until roast is very tender.

2 Place roast on warm platter. Skim and discard fat from cooking liquid. Serve roast with vegetables and sauce.

....

EACH SERVING: ABOUT 360 CALORIES, 25G PROTEIN, 27G CARBOHYDRATE, 21G TOTAL FAT (8G SATURATED), 2G FIBER, 83MG CHOLESTEROL, 540MG SODIUM.

PROVENÇAL Stew

Herbes de Provence is a mixture of marjoram, rosemary, thyme, oregano, and sometimes a dash of lavender that is also delicious in marinades and rubs.

ACTIVE TIME: 30 MINUTES   **COOKING TIME:** 10 HOURS   **MAKES:** 8 MAIN-DISH SERVINGS

1 (4-pound) boneless beef chuck roast, tied

salt and ground black pepper

2 teaspoons vegetable oil

2 pounds carrots, peeled and thinly sliced

1 medium onion (6 to 8 ounces), sliced

3 cloves garlic, minced

2 tablespoons water

1 cup beef broth

½ cup dry white wine

1 teaspoon Herbes de Provence

1 teaspoon fennel seeds

3 strips orange peel

baguette, for serving

1 Rub beef chuck roast with ½ teaspoon each salt and pepper. In 12-inch skillet, heat vegetable oil on medium-high until very hot. Brown on all sides. Transfer to 6- to 7-quart slow cooker bowl.

2 To skillet, add carrots, onion, garlic, water, and ¼ teaspoon salt; cook on medium-high 2 to 4 minutes or until slightly softened, stirring. Add beef broth and wine. Simmer 4 minutes, stirring. Transfer vegetables and liquids to slow cooker bowl along with Herbes de Provence, fennel seeds, and orange peel. Cover; cook 10 hours on Low or until tender.

3 Skim and discard fat from cooking liquid; discard strings. Cut roast into 1-inch cubes. Serve meat with vegetables, cooking liquid, and pieces of baguette.

EACH SERVING: ABOUT 515 CALORIES, 48G PROTEIN, 12G CARBOHYDRATE, 30G TOTAL FAT (12G SATURATED), 3G FIBER, 185MG CHOLESTEROL, 420MG SODIUM.

GINGER AND SOY-BRAISED
Short Ribs

Hours of cooking melt the fat on this cut of beef, creating an intense meatiness that holds its own with Asian spices like star anise. Serve the short ribs with steamed broccoli spears and brown rice.

ACTIVE TIME: 20 MINUTES   **COOKING TIME:** 10 HOURS ON LOW OR 5 HOURS ON HIGH
MAKES: 8 MAIN-DISH SERVINGS

4   pounds bone-in beef short ribs

salt and ground black pepper

2   teaspoons vegetable oil

1   cup beef broth

2   tablespoons reduced-sodium soy sauce

2   tablespoons balsamic vinegar

5   slices (thick) fresh ginger

3   tablespoons brown sugar

2   cloves garlic, smashed

3   star anise pods

sesame seeds, for serving (optional)

chopped green onions, for serving (optional)

1 Sprinkle 4 pounds bone-in beef short ribs with ½ teaspoon each salt and pepper. In 12-inch skillet, heat 2 teaspoons vegetable oil on medium-high until very hot. In batches, brown short ribs just on meaty sides.

2 Meanwhile, in 6- to 7-quart slow cooker bowl, whisk together beef broth, soy sauce, vinegar, ginger, brown sugar, garlic, and star anise. Transfer meat to slow cooker bowl. Cover and cook 10 hours on Low or 5 hours on High, or until very tender. Transfer meat to cutting board. Skim and discard fat from cooking liquid.

3 Transfer cooking liquid to 4-quart saucepot; heat to boiling on medium-high. Boil 5 to 10 minutes or until reduced by about half.

4 To serve, discard ginger, garlic cloves, and star anise. Drizzle meat with reduced sauce; garnish with sesame seeds and green onion slices.

EACH SERVING (WITHOUT RICE AND BROCCOLI): ABOUT 560 CALORIES, 25G PROTEIN, 6G CARBO-HYDRATE, 48G TOTAL FAT (20G SATURATED), 0G FIBER, 107MG CHOLESTEROL, 485MG SODIUM.

SLOW COOKER
Ropa Vieja

The name of this Latin-style braised beef dish literally means "old clothes," because the meat is cooked until it's so tender it can be shredded into what resembles a pile of rags.

ACTIVE TIME: 15 MINUTES   **COOKING TIME:** 9 HOURS   **MAKES:** 10 MAIN-DISH SERVINGS

½ cup drained, sliced pickled jalapeño chiles

3 red, orange, and/or yellow peppers, cut into ¼-inch-wide slices

2 cloves garlic, thinly sliced

1 large onion (12 ounces), cut in half and sliced

1 teaspoon ground cumin

½ teaspoon dried oregano

1 bay leaf

salt

2 (1¾ pounds each) beef flank steaks

1 can (14½ ounces) whole tomatoes in juice

warm tortillas, to serve (optional)

1. In 6- to 6½-quart slow cooker bowl, stir together jalapeños, peppers, garlic, onion, cumin, oregano, bay leaf, and 1 teaspoon salt. Top with flank steaks, cutting steaks if necessary to fit in slow cooker bowl. With kitchen shears, coarsely cut up tomatoes in can. Pour tomatoes with their juice over steaks in slow cooker; do not stir. Cover slow cooker with lid, and cook on Low setting 9 hours.

2. With slotted spoon, transfer steak and vegetables to large bowl. Discard bay leaf. With 2 forks, shred steak, with the grain, into fine strips. Skim and discard fat from cooking liquid. Stir cooking liquid into steak mixture. Spoon into serving bowls, and serve with warm tortillas if you like.

EACH SERVING: ABOUT 300 CALORIES, 36G PROTEIN, 8G CARBOHYDRATE, 13G TOTAL FAT (5G SATURATED), 2G FIBER, 66MG CHOLESTEROL, 455MG SODIUM.

Pot Roast
WITH RED WINE SAUCE

Classic French indgredients like thyme, pearl onions,
and red wine season this easy meal. To recycle leftovers for Pot Roast
Chili, save ⅓ each of beef, vegetables, and cooking liquid in a container;
refrigerate up to 3 days.

ACTIVE TIME: 20 MINUTES   **COOKING TIME:** 10 HOURS   **MAKES:** 8 MAIN-DISH SERVINGS

1   (4½-pound) boneless beef chuck roast, tied

salt and ground black pepper

1   teaspoon vegetable oil

1   pound carrots

1   pound frozen pearl onions

3   cloves garlic, crushed with press

½   teaspoon dried thyme

1   cup dry red wine

1   can (28 ounces) no-salt-added diced
    tomatoes, drained

1   bay leaf

fresh flat-leaf parsley leaves, chopped,
    for garnish

1   With paper towels, pat beef dry; season with
¼ teaspoon each salt and pepper.
2   In 12-inch skillet, heat oil on medium-high.
Add beef and cook 10 to 13 minutes, turning
to brown on all sides. Transfer to 6-quart slow
cooker bowl. While beef browns, peel carrots and
cut into 2-inch chunks. Move to slow cooker bowl.
3   To same skillet, add onions, garlic, and thyme.
Cook 2 minutes or until golden, stirring often.
Add wine; cook 3 minutes, stirring and scraping
up browned bits. Transfer to slow cooker bowl,
along with tomatoes and bay leaf; cover with lid
and cook on Low 10 hours.
4   Transfer beef to cutting board; discard strings.
Move vegetables to serving platter; discard bay
leaf. Transfer cooking liquid from slow cooker
bowl to 8-cup liquid measuring cup; discard fat.
Slice meat across grain and arrange on serving
platter with vegetables. Pour remaining cooking
liquid over it. Garnish with parsley.

EACH SERVING: ABOUT 515 CALORIES, 47G PROTEIN,
11G CARBOHYDRATE, 30G TOTAL FAT (12G SATURATED),
3G FIBER, 181MG CHOLESTEROL, 205MG SODIUM.

Leftover Revamp: To make **Pot Roast Chili**, chop reserved beef and vegetables. Heat **1 teaspoon vegetable oil**, in 5-quart saucepot, on medium. Add **2 cloves garlic**, pressed; **1 tablespoon, plus 1 teaspoon ground cumin**; and **1 teaspoon chili powder**. Cook 2 minutes, stirring. Stir in **2 cans no-salt-added black beans** (15 ounces each), drained and rinsed; **chopped beef and vegetables; reserved cooking liquid**; and **¼ teaspoon salt**. Heat to boiling, then reduce heat to simmer 10 minutes, stirring occasionally. Serve with chopped **fresh cilantro**, **sour cream**, and **lime wedges**. Serves 6.

EACH SERVING: ABOUT 380 CALORIES, 31G PROTEIN, 26G CARBOHYDRATE, 16G TOTAL FAT (6G SATURATED), 9G FIBER, 91MG CHOLESTEROL, 225MG SODIUM.

Chunky Chili
WITH BEANS

A mix of pork and beef adds richness—a bowl of comfort for a cold winter's day. When purchasing chili powder, look for a sodium-free blend. Serve with wedges of cornbread.

ACTIVE TIME: 40 MINUTES **COOKING TIME:** 10 HOURS ON LOW OR 5 HOURS ON HIGH
MAKES: 10 MAIN-DISH SERVINGS

4 slices bacon, cut crosswise into ½-inch pieces

1½ pounds boneless pork shoulder, trimmed and cut into 1-inch chunks

1½ pounds boneless beef chuck, trimmed and cut into 1-inch chunks

1 jumbo onion (about 1 pound), coarsely chopped

¼ cup chili powder

4 cloves (large) garlic, crushed with press

1 tablespoon ground cumin

1½ teaspoons dried oregano

salt

1 can (28 ounces) diced tomatoes

1 cup water

3 cans (15 to 19 ounces each) kidney beans, rinsed and drained

sour cream, to serve (optional)

chopped cilantro, to serve (optional)

1 In 12-inch skillet, cook bacon over medium heat until browned and crisp, stirring occasionally. With slotted spoon, transfer bacon to plate; cover and refrigerate until ready to use. Pour bacon fat into cup and reserve.

2 Increase heat to medium-high; add pork and beef in 3 batches to skillet and cook until well browned. With slotted spoon, remove meat to 5- to 6-quart slow cooker pot as it browns.

3 Return 1 tablespoon bacon fat to skillet; reduce heat to medium. Add onion and cook 8 to 10 minutes or until tender, stirring occasionally. Stir in chili powder, garlic, cumin, oregano, and ½ teaspoon of salt; cook 30 seconds to toast spices. Add tomatoes and water, stirring to scrape up browned bits from bottom of skillet. Remove skillet from heat.

4 To meat in slow cooker, add onion mixture and beans; stir well to combine. Cover slow cooker and cook chili on Low, 8 to 10 hours (or on High 4 to 5 hours) or until meat is fork-tender. Skim and discard any fat from chili. Stir in bacon. Serve with sour cream and cilantro if you like.

EACH SERVING: ABOUT 400 CALORIES, 39G PROTEIN, 31G CARBOHYDRATE, 13G TOTAL FAT (4G SATURATED), 10G FIBER, 101MG CHOLESTEROL, 875MG SODIUM.

BEER-BRAISED
Beef Stew

Use a dark beer like stout, porter, or brown ale to deliver the heartiness needed to match the beef.

ACTIVE TIME: 30 MINUTES **COOKING TIME:** 10 HOURS **MAKES:** 8 MAIN-DISH SERVINGS

1 (4-pound) boneless beef chuck roast, tied

salt and ground black pepper

2 tablespoons vegetable oil

2 medium onions (6 to 8 ounces each), sliced

2 pounds carrots, peeled and sliced

2 tablespoons water

1 bottle (12 ounces) dark beer, such as a brown ale

⅓ cup white (distilled) vinegar

½ cup ketchup

⅓ cup golden raisins

3 tablespoons brown sugar

green beans, for serving (if desired)

1 Rub beef chuck roast with ½ teaspoon each salt and pepper. In 12-inch skillet, heat vegetable oil on medium-high until very hot. Brown roast on all sides. Transfer to 6- to 7-quart slow cooker bowl.

2 To skillet, add onions, carrots, water, and ¼ teaspoon salt; cook on medium-high 2 to 4 minutes or until slightly softened, stirring. Add beer and vinegar. Simmer 4 minutes, stirring. Transfer vegetables and liquids to slow cooker bowl along with ketchup, raisins, and brown sugar. Cover; cook 10 hours on Low or until tender.

3 Skim and discard fat from cooking liquid. Slice meat; serve with vegetables and green beans, if desired. Drizzle with cooking liquid.

EACH SERVING: ABOUT 580 CALORIES, 48G PROTEIN, 28G CARBOHYDRATE, 30G TOTAL FAT (12G SATURATED), 4G FIBER, 185MG CHOLESTEROL, 535MG SODIUM.

Short Ribs
WITH ROOT VEGETABLES

Simmering short ribs with a dry red wine like Pinot Noir, Shiraz/Syrah, or Cabernet Sauvignon provides an acidity that enhances the flavors in the dish.

ACTIVE TIME: 35 MINUTES **COOKING TIME:** 10 HOURS ON LOW OR 5 HOURS ON HIGH
MAKES: 4 MAIN-DISH SERVINGS

3 pounds bone-in beef chuck short ribs

salt and ground black pepper

2 large parsnips (about 4 ounces each), peeled and cut into 1-inch chunks

1 medium turnip (about 8 ounces), peeled and cut into 1-inch chunks

1 bag (16 ounces) carrots, peeled and cut into 2-inch chunks

1 jumbo onion (about 1 pound), coarsely chopped

4 cloves (large) garlic, thinly sliced

1 teaspoon dried thyme

2 cups dry red wine

¼ cup tomato paste

1 Heat 12-inch skillet over medium-high heat until hot. Add ribs to skillet and sprinkle with ½ teaspoon salt and ¼ teaspoon pepper. Cook ribs about 10 minutes or until well browned on all sides, turning occasionally.

2 Meanwhile, in 5- to 6-quart slow cooker pot, place parsnips, turnip, and carrots.

3 Transfer ribs to slow cooker on top of vegetables. Discard drippings in skillet. Reduce heat to medium; add onion and cook about 8 minutes or until browned, stirring frequently. Stir in garlic and thyme and cook 1 minute, stirring constantly. Add wine and heat to boiling over high heat, stirring to loosen browned bits from bottom of skillet. Remove skillet from heat and stir in tomato paste, ½ teaspoon salt, and ¼ teaspoon pepper.

4 Pour wine mixture over ribs in slow cooker. Cover slow cooker with lid and cook on Low, 8 to 10 hours (or on High 4 to 5 hours), or until meat is fork-tender and falling off the bone.

5 With tongs, transfer ribs to deep platter; discard bones if you like. With spoon, skim fat from sauce in slow cooker and discard fat. Spoon vegetables and sauce over ribs.

EACH SERVING: ABOUT 655 CALORIES, 27G PROTEIN, 24G CARBOHYDRATE, 50G TOTAL FAT (21G SATURATED), 5G FIBER, 114MG CHOLESTEROL, 535MG SODIUM.

3-Napkin Baby Back Ribs
 (page 71)

3 Pork & Lamb

There's nothing quite like the aroma of a steaming pot of warming soup. To the rescue are Chunky Ham and Split Pea Soup or Kielbasa Stew. With an easy prep and freeze-ability factor, these soups will make many appearances on the winter dinner menu rotation.

A pork shoulder melds with tart tomatillos in New Mexican Green Chile Pork and cannellini beans turn silky for Lamb Shanks with White Beans and Rosemary. Ribs turn out tender and moist in the slow cooker. Spareribs braise in a homemade sauce in Fall-Off-the-Bone BBQ Ribs, baby back ribs are rubbed in a chile pepper–heavy blend in 3-Napkin Baby Back Ribs, and ribs get the teriyaki treatment in Low-and-Slow Ribs with Asian Cuke Salad. Succulent meat isn't the only winning strategy for these dishes, although we're sure your family will be appreciative. Like most stews, the flavor goes up a notch the next day, making leftovers a hot commodity.

CHUNKY HAM AND SPLIT PEA
Soup

If a less chunky consistency is your soup style, puree it in a food
processor or blender until silky smooth.

ACTIVE TIME: 30 MINUTES   **COOKING TIME:** 10 HOURS ON LOW OR 5 HOURS ON HIGH
MAKES: 6 MAIN-DISH SERVINGS

8 cups water

4 large carrots, peeled and cut into
   ½-inch pieces

3 large stalks celery, cut into ½-inch pieces

2 bay leaves

2 cloves garlic, crushed with press

2 smoked ham hocks (about 1¾ pounds)

1 bag (16 ounces) split green peas, picked
   over, rinsed, and drained

1 small onion (4 to 6 ounces), chopped

½ teaspoon dried thyme

salt

2 tablespoons fresh lemon juice (from
   1 large lemon)

croutons, for serving (optional)

1 In 4½- to 6-quart slow cooker bowl, combine
water, carrots, celery, bay leaves, garlic, ham
hocks, split peas, onion, thyme, and 1 tablespoon
salt. Cover slow cooker with lid and cook on Low
8 to 10 hours or High 4 to 5 hours.

2 With tongs, transfer ham hocks to cutting
board to cool slightly. Discard bay leaves. Keep
soup warm.

3 When ham hocks are cool enough to handle,
discard skin, fat, and bones. Cut meat into small
pieces; return to soup. Stir in lemon juice. Serve
with croutons if desired.

EACH SERVING: ABOUT 350 CALORIES, 24G PROTEIN,
54G CARBOHYDRATE, 5G TOTAL FAT (4G SATURATED),
22G FIBER, 19MG CHOLESTEROL, 1,260MG SODIUM.

Smoked Pork
WITH SAUERKRAUT AND APPLES

Smoked pork shoulder is an under used cut. Its richness is a perfect match for tangy sauerkraut.

ACTIVE TIME: 15 MINUTES   **COOKING TIME:** ABOUT 10 HOURS ON LOW OR 4 HOURS ON HIGH
MAKES: 6 MAIN-DISH SERVINGS

1   small smoked pork shoulder roll (about 2 pounds)

2   pounds small red potatoes (about 8), each cut into quarters

2   large cooking apples, such as Gala or Rome Beauty, unpeeled and cut into 1-inch chunks

2   bay leaves

1   bag (32 ounces) sauerkraut, rinsed and drained

1   clove (large) garlic, sliced

1   small onion, thinly sliced

1   cup white wine

½   teaspoon caraway seeds

Dijon mustard, for serving (optional)

1   Remove netting from pork.

2   In 4½- to 6-quart slow cooker bowl, combine potatoes, apples, bay leaves, sauerkraut, garlic, onion, wine, and caraway seeds. Place pork on top of mixture. Cover slow cooker with lid and cook on Low setting 8 to 10 hours or on High setting 3½ to 4 hours.

3   Discard bay leaves. Carefully transfer pork to cutting board. Cut into slices. Serve with sauerkraut mixture and mustard, if desired.

EACH SERVING: ABOUT 520 CALORIES, 23G PROTEIN, 46G CARBOHYDRATE, 27G TOTAL FAT (9G SATURATED), 8G FIBER, 89MG CHOLESTEROL, 2,325MG SODIUM.

NEW MEXICAN
Green Chile Pork

Picnic shoulder (from the lower part of the pork shoulder)
can also be used in this recipe. To have leftovers for the Green Chile
Pork Tacos, transfer ⅓ of meat and ¼ of the sauce to a container;
refrigerate up to 3 days.

ACTIVE TIME: 25 MINUTES   **COOKING TIME:** ABOUT 8 HOURS   **MAKES:** 8 MAIN-DISH SERVINGS

1   (4-pound) bone-in pork shoulder roast
    (Boston butt)

1   tablespoon chipotle chile powder

1   tablespoon packed brown sugar

salt and ground black pepper

2   pounds fresh tomatillos, husked, rinsed, and
    each cut in half

1   jumbo white onion (1 pound), cut into 1-inch
    chunks

4   cloves garlic, peeled

3   jalapeño chiles, each cut in half, seeds and
    ribs removed

½   cup packed fresh cilantro with stems, plus
    leaves for garnish

⅓   cup low-sodium chicken broth

3   cups cooked brown rice, for serving

lime wedges, for serving

cilantro leaves, for garnish

1   Arrange oven rack 6 inches from broiler heat source. Preheat broiler. Line 18-inch by 12-inch jelly-roll pan with foil.

2   Place pork in 6-quart slow cooker bowl. In small bowl, combine chile powder, sugar, 1 teaspoon salt, and ½ teaspoon ground black pepper. Rub all over pork in bowl.

3   On prepared pan, spread tomatillos, onion, garlic, and jalapeños in single layer. Broil 7 minutes or until blackened and blistered in spots, stirring twice. Immediately add to slow cooker bowl along with cilantro and broth. Cover with lid and cook on Low 8 hours.

4   With tongs and large serving spoon, transfer pork to cutting board. Remove and discard bone and excess fat. With large serving spoon, transfer all vegetables to blender. Puree until smooth. Thin with additional cooking liquid if desired. Discard remaining liquid in slow cooker bowl.

5   Cut pork in slices across grain. Divide among serving plates, along with rice and lime wedges. Spoon remaining sauce over pork and garnish with cilantro leaves.

EACH SERVING: ABOUT 440 CALORIES, 29G PROTEIN, 34G CARBOHYDRATE, 21G TOTAL FAT (7G SATURATED), 5G FIBER, 99MG CHOLESTEROL, 350MG SODIUM.

Leftover Revamp: To make **Green Chile Pork Tacos**, combine **1 bunch radishes (12 ounces)**, chopped; **¼ cup fresh cilantro**, finely chopped; **1 tablespoon fresh lime juice**; and **¼ teaspoon salt** in bowl. Cut **reserved pork** into 1-inch chunks. Heat **½ teaspoon vegetable oil** in 12-inch skillet, on medium. Add pork and cook 4 to 5 minutes or until browned and hot, stirring and scraping up browned bits. Add **½ cup reserved sauce** and cook 1 to 2 minutes or until heated through, stirring. Divide among **12 corn tortillas**, warmed; top with radish mixture. Serve with sauce and **lime wedges**. Serves 6.

EACH SERVING: ABOUT 305 CALORIES, 17G PROTEIN, 33G CARBOHYDRATE, 13G TOTAL FAT (4G SATURATED), 50MG CHOLESTEROL, 320MG SODIUM.

FALL-OFF-THE-BONE
BBQ Ribs

If you crave a smoky taste without a punch of heat, welcome the allure of smoked paprika, made from grinding smoked sweet red peppers.

ACTIVE TIME: 15 MINUTES   **COOKING TIME:** 10 HOURS ON LOW OR 5 HOURS ON HIGH
MAKES: 6 MAIN-DISH SERVINGS

1   medium onion (6 to 8 ounces), chopped

½   cup ketchup

¼   cup cider vinegar

¼   cup packed brown sugar

¼   cup tomato paste

2   tablespoons paprika or smoked paprika

2   tablespoons Worcestershire sauce

1   tablespoon yellow mustard

salt and ground black pepper

4   pounds pork spareribs

1 In 4½- to 6-quart slow cooker bowl, stir onion, ketchup, vinegar, sugar, tomato paste, paprika, Worcestershire sauce, mustard, 1 teaspoon salt, and 1 teaspoon pepper until combined. Add ribs, cutting into several large pieces to fit in slow cooker bowl. Spoon sauce over and around ribs to coat. Cover slow cooker with lid and cook on Low setting 8 to 10 hours or on High setting 4 to 5 hours.

2 Transfer ribs to platter. Skim and discard fat from cooking liquid. Spoon remaining liquid over ribs.

....

EACH SERVING: ABOUT 560 CALORIES, 39G PROTEIN, 23G CARBOHYDRATE, 34G TOTAL FAT (13G SATURATED), 2G FIBER, 136MG CHOLESTEROL, 873MG SODIUM.

Baby Back Ribs

These ribs are so juicy and tender that serving them with at least three napkins is an absolute must. To intensify the muy caliente level, double the amount of crushed red pepper. Use kitchen shears to cut the ribs with ease. For photo, see page 64.

ACTIVE TIME: 15 MINUTES   **COOKING TIME:** 7 HOURS ON LOW OR 4 HOURS ON HIGH
MAKES: 8 MAIN-DISH SERVINGS

2   tablespoons chili powder

2   tablespoons smoked paprika

1   tablespoon brown sugar

1   tablespoon onion powder

salt and ground black pepper

2   racks (about 4 to 5 pounds) baby back pork ribs

1   cup ketchup

¼   cup Worcestershire sauce

3   tablespoons cider vinegar

3   tablespoons molasses

2   teaspoons crushed red pepper

1 In medium bowl, combine chili powder, paprika, brown sugar, onion powder, 1 teaspoon salt, and ½ teaspoon black pepper. Cut racks of ribs into sets of 3 bones. Rub spices all over ribs.

2 In 7- to 8-quart slow cooker bowl, whisk ketchup, Worcestershire sauce, vinegar, molasses, and crushed red pepper. Add ribs to bowl, bone-sides down; do not submerge. Cover with lid; cook on Low 7 hours or on High 4 hours, or until tender.

3 When ready to serve, arrange oven rack 5 to 6 inches from broiler heat source; preheat on high. Transfer ribs to large, foil-lined jelly-roll pan. Pour cooking liquid into fat separator; discard fat. Brush liquid all over ribs. Broil ribs 2 to 3 minutes or until slightly charred. Brush with liquid again before serving.

EACH SERVING: ABOUT 400 CALORIES, 26G PROTEIN, 20G CARBOHYDRATE, 24G TOTAL FAT (9G SATURATED), 2G FIBER, 92MG CHOLESTEROL, 895MG SODIUM.

Low-and-Slow Ribs
WITH ASIAN CUKE SALAD

You'll need eight hours to slow cook pork spareribs (on low), but the reward for your patience will be delectable. Our test kitchen got hearty, stick-to-the-ribs results using a thicker style of teriyaki glaze like Kikkoman's Teriyaki Baste & Glaze rather than a thinner sauce.

ACTIVE TIME: 20 MINUTES   **COOKING TIME:** 8 HOURS ON LOW OR 4 HOURS ON HIGH
MAKES: 8 MAIN-DISH SERVINGS

3½ pounds pork spareribs

1   cup teriyaki glaze

1   English (seedless) cucumber (12 to 14 ounces), peeled and thinly sliced

1   bag (10 ounces) shredded carrots

¼   cup seasoned rice vinegar

1   In 4½- to 6-quart slow cooker bowl, place ribs and teriyaki glaze, spreading teriyaki to coat ribs on all sides. Cover slow cooker with lid and cook on Low setting 8 hours or on High setting 4 hours.

2   Meanwhile, in medium bowl, stir cucumber, carrots, and rice vinegar until combined. Cover and refrigerate until ready to serve.

3   To serve, transfer ribs to cutting board; cut into portions. Skim and discard fat from cooking liquid. Arrange ribs and salad on dinner plates. Spoon remaining liquid over ribs.

EACH SERVING: ABOUT 390 CALORIES, 26G PROTEIN, 18G CARBOHYDRATE, 22G TOTAL FAT (9G SATURATED), 1G FIBER, 89MG CHOLESTEROL, 1,185MG SODIUM.

PULLED PORK
Sandwiches

This meltingly tender pork is simmered for hours in a sweet and tangy sauce before shredding.

ACTIVE TIME: 15 MINUTES   COOKING TIME: 10 HOURS   MAKES: 12 MAIN-DISH SERVINGS

1   medium onion (6 to 8 ounces), chopped

½   cup ketchup

⅓   cup cider vinegar

¼   cup packed brown sugar

¼   cup tomato paste

2   tablespoons sweet paprika

2   tablespoons Worcestershire sauce

2   tablespoons yellow mustard

salt and ground black pepper

4   pounds boneless pork shoulder blade roast (fresh pork butt), cut into 4 pieces

12 soft sandwich buns or ciabatta rolls, warmed

dill pickles, for serving (optional)

potato chips, for serving (optional)

hot sauce, for serving (optional)

1 In 4½- to 6-quart slow cooker bowl, stir onion, ketchup, vinegar, brown sugar, tomato paste, paprika, Worcestershire sauce, mustard, 1½ teaspoon salt, and 1¼ teaspoon pepper until combined. Add pork to sauce mixture and turn to coat well with sauce.

2 Cover slow cooker with lid and cook on Low setting, 8 to 10 hours or until pork is very tender.

3 With tongs, transfer pork to large bowl. Turn slow cooker to High; cover and heat sauce to boiling to thicken and reduce slightly. While sauce boils, with 2 forks, pull pork into shreds. Return shredded pork to slow cooker and toss with sauce to combine. Cover slow cooker and heat through on High setting, if necessary.

4 Spoon pork mixture onto bottom of sandwich buns; replace tops of buns. Serve sandwiches with pickles, potato chips, and hot sauce if you like.

EACH SERVING: ABOUT 475 CALORIES, 31G PROTEIN, 29G CARBOHYDRATE, 26G TOTAL FAT (9G SATURATED), 2G FIBER, 107MG CHOLESTEROL, 760MG SODIUM.

KIELBASA **Stew**

A protein-rich hearty soup for cold winter nights. Better yet?
Lentils boast a hefty amount of cholesterol-lowering fiber.

ACTIVE TIME: 20 MINUTES   **COOKING TIME:** 10 HOURS ON LOW OR 6 HOURS ON HIGH
MAKES: 6 MAIN-DISH SERVINGS

2   teaspoons vegetable oil

1   small yellow onion (6 to 8 ounces), sliced

2   stalks celery, sliced

1   teaspoon caraway seeds

3   bay leaves

salt

1   pound Yukon gold potatoes

2   cups dried lentils, rinsed

4   cups low-sodium chicken broth

1   cup apple cider

14 ounces kielbasa, thinly sliced

1   cup sauerkraut, drained

grainy mustard, for serving (optional)

parsley leaves, for garnish (optional)

1 In 12-inch skillet, heat vegetable oil on
medium. Add onion, celery, caraway seeds, bay
leaves, and ¼ teaspoon salt. Cook 1 to 3 minutes
or until slightly softened, stirring frequently.
Transfer to 6- to 7-quart slow cooker bowl.

2 To slow cooker bowl, add potatoes, lentils,
chicken broth, cider, and kielbasa. Cover and
cook 9 to 10 hours on Low or 6 hours on High,
or until lentils are tender.

3 Discard bay leaves. Into slow cooker bowl, stir
in sauerkraut. Serve with grainy mustard and
garnish with parsley, if desired.

EACH SERVING: ABOUT 430 CALORIES, 30G PROTEIN,
67G CARBOHYDRATE, 5G TOTAL FAT (1G SATURATED),
17G FIBER, 23MG CHOLESTEROL, 895MG SODIUM.

TOMATILLO **Pork**

For this recipe, pork is simmered with salsa verde,
a green salsa made of tomatillos, green chiles, and cilantro,
typically found in a range of heat levels.

ACTIVE TIME: 10 MINUTES   **COOKING TIME:** 10 HOURS ON LOW OR 5½ HOURS ON HIGH
MAKES: 5 MAIN-DISH SERVINGS

1   large bunch cilantro

3   garlic cloves, sliced

2   pounds small red potatoes (about 8), each cut
into quarters

1   bone-in pork shoulder roast (about 3 pounds),
well-trimmed

1   jar (16 to 18 ounces) salsa verde (green salsa)

1   From bunch of cilantro, remove 15 large sprigs. Remove enough leaves from remaining cilantro to equal ½ cup, loosely packed. Refrigerate leaves to sprinkle over pork after cooking.

2   In 4½- to 6-quart slow cooker bowl, combine cilantro sprigs, garlic, and potatoes. Place pork on top of potato mixture. Pour salsa over and around pork. Cover slow cooker with lid and cook on Low setting 8 to 10 hours or on High setting 5 to 5½ hours.

3   Transfer pork and potatoes to warm deep platter. Discard cilantro sprigs. Skim and discard fat from cooking liquid. Spoon cooking liquid over pork and potatoes. Coarsely chop reserved ½ cup cilantro leaves; sprinkle over pork.

....

EACH SERVING: ABOUT 300 CALORIES, 25G PROTEIN, 27G CARBOHYDRATE, 9G TOTAL FAT (3G SATURATED), 2G FIBER, 79MG CHOLESTEROL, 295MG SODIUM.

Lamb Shanks
WITH WHITE BEANS AND ROSEMARY

White beans and rosemary (whether dried or fresh) are a delectable combo, especially when paired with luscious lamb.

ACTIVE TIME: 20 MINUTES   **COOKING TIME:** 10 HOURS ON LOW OR 6 HOURS ON HIGH
MAKES: 6 MAIN-DISH SERVINGS

4   garlic cloves, crushed with press

3   large carrots, peeled and cut into ½-inch-thick rounds

2   cans (15 to 19 ounces each) white kidney beans (cannellini), rinsed and drained

2   sprigs fresh rosemary plus additional for garnish

2   tablespoons tomato paste

1   large onion (about 12 ounces), cut into 8 wedges

½   cup chicken broth or water

1   cup dry white wine

salt and ground black pepper

6   small lamb shanks (about 1 pound each)

1 In a 4½- to 6-quart slow cooker bowl, combine garlic, carrots, beans, rosemary, tomato paste, onion, broth, wine, 2 teaspoons salt, and 1 teaspoon pepper. Place lamb on top of vegetables. Cover slow cooker with lid and cook on Low setting 8 to 10 hours or on High setting 5 to 6 hours.

2 With tongs, transfer lamb shanks to large serving bowl. Remove and discard rosemary. Skim and discard fat from liquid.

3 If you prefer a thicker sauce, with slotted spoon, transfer about 1 cup bean-and-vegetable mixture to small bowl and coarsely mash with fork or potato masher. Return bean mixture to slow cooker bowl; stir until well mixed. Spoon bean mash around lamb shanks. Garnish with rosemary sprigs.

EACH SERVING: ABOUT 555 CALORIES, 49G PROTEIN, 34G CARBOHYDRATE, 24G TOTAL FAT (10G SATURATED), 9G FIBER, 151MG CHOLESTEROL, 1,250MG SODIUM.

ZESTY PORK **Tacos**

Prepare the meat in the morning and come home to tasty and spicy tacos, with this easy make-ahead meal.

ACTIVE TIME: 25 MINUTES   **COOKING TIME:** 10 HOURS ON LOW OR 7 HOURS ON HIGH
MAKES: 12 MAIN-DISH SERVINGS

3   tablespoons chopped chipotles in adobo

2   teaspoons chili powder

1   teaspoon grated lime peel

salt and ground black pepper

1   (4- to 5-pound) boneless pork shoulder (Boston butt)

½   cup ketchup

¼   cup orange juice

2   tablespoons Worcestershire sauce

¼   teaspoon ground cinnamon

1   medium onion (6 to 8 ounces), chopped

2   cloves garlic, chopped

flour tortillas (soft-taco size), for serving

shredded green cabbage, for serving

sliced radishes, for serving

cilantro, for serving

lime wedges, for serving

1 In small bowl, combine chopped chipotles in adobo, chili powder, and lime peel with ½ teaspoon each salt and pepper. Cut pork shoulder into 4 equal pieces. Season with rub mixture.

2 In 6- to 7-quart slow cooker bowl, whisk together ketchup, orange juice, Worcestershire sauce, cinnamon, and ¼ teaspoon each salt and pepper; add onion and garlic. Place meat on top of vegetables in slow cooker bowl.

3 Cover and cook 10 hours on Low or 7 hours on High, or until very tender. Transfer meat to cutting board. Skim and discard fat from cooking liquid.

4 With hands, shred meat (discard fat and gristle). Return meat to slow cooker bowl with sauce. Serve meat with flour tortillas, shredded green cabbage, sliced radishes, cilantro, and lime wedges.

EACH SERVING: ABOUT 410 CALORIES, 31G PROTEIN, 31G CARBOHYDRATE, 18G TOTAL FAT (6G SATURATED), 2G FIBER, 100MG CHOLESTEROL, 730MG SODIUM.

Tuscan Pork
WITH FENNEL

Its bargain price makes pork shoulder a staple at big-crowd barbecues, but the fork-tender meat also marries well with Italian spices. Save a few fennel fronds, chopping them to use as garnish.

ACTIVE TIME: 25 MINUTES   **COOKING TIME:** 10 HOURS ON LOW OR 7 HOURS ON HIGH
MAKES: 12 MAIN-DISH SERVINGS

2   teaspoons fennel seeds

1   teaspoon dried rosemary

salt and ground black pepper

1   (4- to 5-pound) boneless pork shoulder (Boston butt)

3/4   cup chicken broth

2   teaspoons chicken broth base or demi-glace

2   pounds red potatoes, sliced

2   medium fennel bulbs, cored and cut into wedges

3   cloves garlic, chopped

1 In small bowl, combine fennel seeds, rosemary, and ½ teaspoon each salt and pepper. Cut boneless pork shoulder into 4 equal pieces. Season with rub mixture.

2 In 6- to 7-quart slow cooker bowl, whisk together chicken broth base/demi-glace, and ¼ teaspoon each salt and pepper; add potatoes, fennel, and garlic. Place meat on top of vegetables in slow cooker bowl.

3 Cover and cook 10 hours on Low or 7 hours on High, or until very tender. Transfer meat to cutting board. Skim and discard fat from cooking liquid.

4 Slice pork and serve with vegetables. Drizzle with cooking liquid. Garnish with chopped fennel fronds, if desired.

EACH SERVING: ABOUT 355 CALORIES, 29G PROTEIN, 104G CARBOHYDRATE, 19G TOTAL FAT (7G SATURATED), 3G FIBER, 104MG CHOLESTEROL, 350MG SODIUM.

Chipotle Pork
(page 94)

4 | Pasta

While slow cooker and pasta aren't words that necessarily go hand in hand, this chapter will guide you on why they should. Let's face it—there's no better meal option for busy weeknights than pasta, except, of course, when you can pair it with an all-day simmering sauce, like Big-Batch Tomato Sauce.

Discover the genius of spaghetti noodles cooked straight in the slow cooker, soaking up the liquid goodness in Southwestern Chicken Stew. Vegetarian Lasagna will make you banish the more time-consuming, oven-baked layered dish. Yet these recipes aren't the only ones to get the slow cooker pasta treatment. Go Asian with red curry-spiked Thai Chicken and Noodles or bask in the regional joy of Cincinnati Chili. Whether as a winter comfort or a way to skip the heat of the oven in summer, these slow cooker recipes are a blueprint for dinners the whole family will adore.

FAMILY-FRIENDLY
Meatballs

A classic Italian recipe the whole family is sure to love. Any leftover meatballs can be layered onto split Italian rolls, smothered with tomato sauce and topped with mozzarella cheese to melt in the oven.

ACTIVE TIME: 25 MINUTES **COOKING TIME:** 6 HOURS ON LOW OR 4 HOURS ON HIGH
MAKES: 8 MAIN-DISH SERVINGS

1 can (28 ounces) crushed tomatoes

½ cup Burgundy or Pinot Noir wine

1 can (6 ounces) tomato paste

1 tablespoon sugar

1 medium onion (6 to 8 ounces) chopped

3 cloves garlic, crushed with press

salt and ground black pepper

1 pound (85 percent lean) ground beef

1 pound ground pork

⅓ cup Italian-seasoned bread crumbs

1 large egg

¼ cup whole milk

¼ cup grated Pecorino Romano Parmesan cheese, plus more for serving

¼ teaspoon crushed red pepper

1½ pounds spaghetti, cooked

1 In 5- to 6-quart slow cooker bowl, combine crushed tomatoes, wine, tomato paste, sugar, onion, and garlic, along with ½ teaspoon each salt and pepper.

2 In large bowl, combine ground beef, ground pork, bread crumbs, egg, whole milk, grated Pecorino Romano cheese, crushed red pepper, and ½ teaspoon each salt and pepper.

3 Using small scoop or rounded tablespoon measure, scoop meat into twenty-four 1½-inch balls; place in slow cooker bowl.

4 Cover and cook 6 hours on Low or 4 hours on High. Transfer meatballs to large bowl. Skim and discard fat from sauce. Serve sauce and meatballs with cooked spaghetti and additional grated Pecorino.

EACH SERVING: ABOUT 654 CALORIES, 38G PROTEIN, 83G CARBOHYDRATE, 18G TOTAL FAT (7 SATURATED), 7G FIBER, 100MG CHOLESTEROL, 723MG SODIUM.

BIG-BATCH **Tomato Sauce**

It is easy to make your own tomato sauce and is even simpler when you use a slow cooker. Make this rich sauce for a crowd or freeze some for later use.

ACTIVE TIME: 20 MINUTES   **COOKING TIME:** 8 HOURS ON LOW OR 4 HOURS ON HIGH
MAKES: 12 MAIN-DISH SERVINGS

8   ounces thick-cut pancetta or bacon, chopped

2   medium red onions (6 to 8 ounces each), thinly sliced

2   cloves garlic, crushed with press

½   teaspoon dried oregano

½   teaspoon crushed red pepper

salt and ground black pepper

4   cans (28 ounces each) whole peeled tomatoes

¼   cup tomato paste

grated Pecorino Romano cheese, for serving

1 In 12-inch skillet, cook pancetta on medium-high 8 minutes or until crisp, stirring occasionally; with slotted spoon, transfer to bowl. To same skillet, add onions, garlic, oregano, red pepper, and ½ teaspoon each salt and black pepper. Reduce heat to medium. Cook 4 minutes or until onions begin to soften, stirring often.

2 Drain 2 cans of tomatoes. In 7- to 8-quart slow cooker bowl, combine drained tomatoes with undrained tomatoes; crush with hands. Add tomato paste, pancetta, onion mixture, and 1 teaspoon salt. Cover with lid; cook on Low 8 hours or on High 4 hours.

3 Serve over cooked pasta, chicken, or pork. Garnish with Pecorino Romano cheese. Sauce can be frozen in airtight containers up to 3 months.

....

EACH SERVING: ABOUT 115 CALORIES, 5G PROTEIN, 5G CARBOHYDRATE, 5G TOTAL FAT (2G SATURATED), 2G FIBER, 14MG CHOLESTEROL, 925MG SODIUM.

VEGETARIAN **Lasagna**

Everyone loves lasagna, but who likes all the hard work? An easier way: Layer no-boil noodles, sauce, frozen spinach, and shredded cheese in your slow cooker. Veggie crumbles stand in for ground beef to cut the fat without losing the protein. *Buon appetito!*

ACTIVE TIME: 15 MINUTES   **COOKING TIME:** 3 HOURS ON LOW OR 1¾ HOURS ON HIGH
MAKES: 8 MAIN-DISH SERVINGS

1   jar (25 to 26 ounces) marinara sauce

1   can (14½ ounces) diced tomatoes

1   package (8 to 9 ounces) oven-ready (no-boil) lasagna noodles

1   container (15 ounces) part-skim ricotta cheese

1   package (8 ounces) shredded Italian cheese blend or shredded mozzarella cheese

1   package (10 ounces) frozen chopped spinach, thawed and squeezed dry

1   cup frozen veggie crumbles (see Tip below)

1   In medium bowl, combine marinara sauce and tomatoes with their juice.

2   Spray 4½- to 6-quart slow cooker bowl with nonstick cooking spray. Spoon 1 cup tomato-sauce mixture into bowl. Arrange ¼ of noodles over sauce, overlapping noodles and breaking into large pieces to cover as much sauce as possible. Spoon about ¾ cup sauce over noodles, then top with ⅓ of ricotta (about ½ cup), and ½ cup shredded cheese. Spread ½ of spinach over cheese.

3   Repeat layering 2 more times beginning with noodles, but in middle layer, replace spinach with frozen crumbles. Place remaining noodles over spinach, then top with remaining sauce and shredded cheese.

4   Cover slow cooker with lid and cook on Low setting 2½ to 3 hours or on High setting 1½ to 1¾ hours or until noodles are very tender.

....

EACH SERVING: ABOUT 425 CALORIES, 24G PROTEIN, 41G CARBOHYDRATE, 17G TOTAL FAT (8G SATURATED), 6G FIBER, 37MG CHOLESTEROL, 1,120MG SODIUM.

TIP

Veggie crumbles are a heat-and-serve vegetarian meat substitute found in your grocer's freezer. If you prefer, substitute 8 ounces browned ground beef for the crumbles.

CINCINNATI **Chili**

Cincinnati has its own unique take on chili: It's served over spaghetti. Tailor the chili to your pantry and tastes—use kidney beans if they're on the shelf and ground turkey if you're cutting back on red meat; halve the amount of chipotle for a less fiery flavor.

ACTIVE TIME: 5 MINUTES   **COOKING TIME:** 6 HOURS   **MAKES:** 6 MAIN-DISH SERVINGS

1½ pounds (92 percent lean) ground beef

1   can (15 ounces) kidney beans, rinsed and drained

1   can (15 ounces) tomato sauce

1   medium onion (6 to 8 ounces), chopped

2   tablespoons brown sugar

2   tablespoons unsweetened cocoa

2   teaspoons ground chipotle chile

2   teaspoons ground cumin

1½ teaspoons ground cinnamon

salt and ground black pepper

1   pound spaghetti, cooked

4   ounces sharp Cheddar cheese, shredded

4   green onions, thinly sliced

1 In 7- to 8-quart slow cooker bowl, combine beef, beans, tomato sauce, onion, brown sugar, cocoa, chipotle, cumin, cinnamon, and ½ teaspoon each salt and black pepper; stir together, breaking up ground beef. Cover with lid and cook on Low 6 hours.

2 When ready to serve, spoon chili over spaghetti. Top with Cheddar and green onions.

EACH SERVING: ABOUT 655 CALORIES, 44G PROTEIN, 81G CARBOHYDRATE, 17G TOTAL FAT (8G SATURATED), 10G FIBER, 89MG CHOLESTEROL, 885MG SODIUM.

TIP

This is equally delish over tortilla chips or baked potatoes in place of the noodles.

Chipotle Pork

Peanut butter and a dash of cocoa powder aren't just a divine dessert combo—they add unique depth of flavor to this tender-cooked pork shoulder. Canned chipotles add smoke and heat. Puree the extras and keep in fridge to mix with a variety of foods like sour cream, mayonnaise, marinades, and salad dressings. For photo, see page 84.

ACTIVE TIME: 15 MINUTES   **COOKING TIME:** 9 HOURS ON LOW OR 6 HOURS ON HIGH
MAKES: 8 MAIN-DISH SERVINGS

1   medium onion (6 to 8 ounces), quartered

½   cup chicken broth

½   cup ketchup

¼   cup chipotles in adobo

¼   cup creamy peanut butter

5   cloves garlic

2   tablespoons cocoa powder

salt

1   boneless pork shoulder (about 3 to 4 pounds), quartered

cooked curly egg noodles, for serving

orange wedges, for garnish

green onions, for garnish

1   In a food processor with knife blade attached, blend onion, chicken broth, ketchup, chipotles, peanut butter, garlic, and cocoa.

2   Season the pork shoulder with 1 teaspoon salt and add into a 6- to 7-quart slow cooker bowl. Pour onion mixture over pork. Cook 8 to 9 hours on Low or 5 to 6 hours on High until pork is tender but not falling apart.

3   Transfer pork to cutting board. Pour sauce into fat separator. When pork is cool enough to handle, remove and discard fat from it.

4   Pull pork into bite-size chunks. Serve over curly egg noodles along with sauce. Garnish with orange wedges and green onions.

EACH SERVING: ABOUT 300 CALORIES, 26G PROTEIN, 14G CARBOHYDRATE, 16G TOTAL FAT (5G SATURATED), 3G FIBER, 104MG CHOLESTEROL, 655MG SODIUM.

THAI
Chicken and Noodles

A spicy marinade adds extra zing to the poultry, while red curry and coconut milk give a richness to this slow-cooked dinner. Look for the Thai red curry paste in the Asian/international aisle of the grocery store, usually not far from the coconut milk.

ACTIVE TIME: 25 MINUTES   **COOKING TIME:** 5 HOURS, PLUS MARINATING
MAKES: 8 MAIN-DISH SERVINGS

2½ pounds bone-in skinless chicken thighs

3   tablespoons Thai red curry paste

½   teaspoon freshly grated lime peel

salt and ground black pepper

1   can (15 ounces) coconut milk

¼   cup peanut butter

2   tablespoons reduced-sodium soy sauce

1   pound green beans, trimmed and cut into 1-inch lengths

1   large shallot, chopped

8   ounces rice noodles, cooked

chopped, roasted unsalted peanuts, for serving

fresh cilantro, for serving

lime wedges, for serving

1 In gallon-size resealable plastic bag, combine chicken thighs with 1 tablespoon red curry paste, grated lime peel, and ½ teaspoon each salt and pepper; refrigerate overnight.

2 In 6- to 7-quart slow cooker bowl, combine coconut milk, peanut butter, soy sauce, green beans, shallot, and remaining 2 tablespoons red curry paste. Place chicken in slow cooker bowl on top of vegetables. Cover and cook 5 hours on Low or until chicken is cooked through (165°F).

3 Transfer chicken to cutting board. Skim and discard fat from cooking liquid. Stir ¼ teaspoon salt into cooking liquid. Pull meat from bones (discard fat, bones, and gristle); return to slow cooker bowl. Toss with cooked rice noodles. Serve with chopped roasted unsalted peanuts, fresh cilantro, and lime wedges.

EACH SERVING: ABOUT 455 CALORIES, 25G PROTEIN, 34G CARBOHYDRATE, 26G TOTAL FAT (13G SATURATED), 3G FIBER, 70MG CHOLESTEROL, 580MG SODIUM.

MEDITERRANEAN **Beef Stew**

Dried apricots sweeten this coriander-spiked classic, but dried dates or golden raisins will also do the trick. An easy way to add flavor and freshness—toss cooked noodles with ¼ cup chopped mint leaves before serving. In a hurry? Serve the stew over couscous instead of pasta to save 5 minutes.

ACTIVE TIME: 30 MINUTES   **COOKING TIME:** 8 HOURS ON LOW OR 5 HOURS ON HIGH
MAKES: 8 MAIN-DISH SERVINGS

¼ cup vegetable oil

1 (about 4 pounds) beef bottom round roast, trimmed and cut into 1-inch cubes

salt and ground black pepper

¾ cup dry white wine

¼ cup all-purpose flour

2 medium onions (6 to 8 ounces), sliced

1 pound carrots, peeled and cut into ½-inch chunks

1½ cups chicken or beef broth

½ cup dried apricots, sliced

1 teaspoon crushed red pepper

1 teaspoon ground coriander

1 lemon

2 medium zucchini, thinly sliced into half-moons

1½ cups pitted green olives

cooked curly egg noodles, for serving

1 In 12-inch skillet, heat 2 tablespoons oil on medium-high. Pat beef dry with paper towels; sprinkle with ½ teaspoon each salt and pepper. In batches, brown beef on two sides, adding remaining oil as needed. Transfer beef to 6- to 8-quart slow cooker bowl.

2 In medium bowl, stir together wine and flour. In same skillet, cook onions on medium 1 minute, stirring. Add wine mixture. Simmer 3 minutes or until thickened, stirring; add to beef. Stir in carrots, broth, apricots, crushed red pepper, and coriander. With peeler, remove 4 large strips peel from lemon; add strips to slow cooker and reserve lemon for later use. Cover; cook on Low 8 hours, on High 5 hours, or until beef is tender. Discard lemon peel.

3 From lemon, squeeze 2 tablespoons juice; stir into stew with zucchini, olives, and ½ teaspoon salt; serve over noodles. Garnish with lemon curls.

....

EACH SERVING (WITHOUT NOODLES): ABOUT 475 CALORIES, 53G PROTEIN, 20G CARBOHYDRATE, 21G TOTAL FAT (4G SATURATED), 139MG CHOLESTEROL, 995MG SODIUM.

RED WINE-BRAISED
Short Ribs

This flavorful short rib recipe is perfect for any dinner party or decadent night in, especially when served with more of the dry red wine. Demi-glace is beef stock that has been simmered until reduced, resulting in a thick, rich glaze with concentrated beef flavor.

ACTIVE TIME: 20 MINUTES   **COOKING TIME:** 10 HOURS ON LOW OR 5 HOURS ON HIGH
MAKES: 8 MAIN-DISH SERVINGS

4   pounds bone-in beef short ribs

salt and ground black pepper

2   teaspoons vegetable oil

1½ cups Burgundy or Pinot Noir wine

1   tablespoon beef broth concentrate
    or demi-glace

2   tablespoons tomato paste

2   dried bay leaves

½   teaspoon dried thyme

1½ pounds carrots, peeled and cut into
    2-inch sticks

8   ounces portobello mushroom caps, chopped

cooked curly egg noodles, for serving

chopped parsley, for serving

1 Sprinkle 4 pounds bone-in beef short ribs with ½ teaspoon each salt and pepper. In 12-inch skillet, heat vegetable oil on medium-high until very hot. In batches, brown short ribs just on meaty sides.

2 Meanwhile, in 6- to 7-quart slow cooker bowl, whisk together wine, concentrate/demi-glace, tomato paste, bay leaves, and thyme; add carrots and mushrooms. Transfer meat to slow cooker bowl.

3 Cover and cook 10 hours on Low or 5 hours on High, or until very tender. Transfer meat to cutting board. Skim and discard fat from cooking liquid.

4 Transfer cooking liquid to 4-quart saucepot; heat to boiling on medium-high. Boil 5 to 10 minutes or until reduced by about half.

5 To Serve: Remove and discard bay leaves. Serve meat and vegetables on top of egg noodles. Drizzle with reduced sauce and chopped parsley.

EACH SERVING (WITHOUT NOODLES): ABOUT 590 CALORIES, 29G PROTEIN, 11G CARBOHYDRATE, 29G TOTAL FAT (20G SATURATED), 3G FIBER, 107MG CHOLESTEROL, 370MG SODIUM.

HERBED
Turkey Thighs
AND ORZO

Infused with all the flavors of fall, this Greek-inspired dish stars lean turkey. Rosemary, oregano, and cumin partner with lemon to add richness without fat. To make our leftover revamp, reserve half the herb mixture and 2 turkey thighs in a container; refrigerate for up to 3 days.

ACTIVE TIME: 20 MINUTES   **COOKING TIME:** 7 HOURS ON LOW OR 5 HOURS ON HIGH
MAKES: 6 MAIN-DISH SERVINGS

1   tablespoon olive oil

6   bone-in turkey thighs (6 to 8 pounds total), skin removed

salt and ground black pepper

1   cup low-sodium chicken broth

1   sprig fresh rosemary

4   cloves garlic, smashed

1   teaspoon cumin seeds

½   teaspoon dried oregano

1½ cups dry red wine

2   tablespoons freshly grated lemon peel

2   tablespoons chopped fresh dill

2   tablespoons chopped fresh parsley

1½ cups cooked orzo

1 In 12-inch skillet, heat oil on medium-high until hot. Sprinkle turkey thighs with 1 teaspoon salt and ½ teaspoon ground black pepper. In batches, add turkey to skillet; cook 7 to 8 minutes or until browned, turning once. Transfer to 6-quart slow cooker bowl, along with broth and rosemary.

2 To same skillet, add garlic, cumin, and oregano. Cook 30 seconds, stirring. Add wine; cook 3 minutes or until wine is reduced by half, stirring and scraping up browned bits. Pour contents of skillet into slow cooker. Cover with lid; cook on Low 7 hours or on High 5 hours.

3 In small bowl, combine lemon peel, dill, and parsley. Divide turkey thighs among serving plates. Garnish with herb mixture. Transfer cooking liquid to fat separator; discard fat. In medium bowl, toss orzo with ⅓ cup cooking liquid. Serve with remaining cooking liquid.

EACH SERVING: ABOUT 575 CALORIES, 72G PROTEIN, 35G CARBOHYDRATE, 14G TOTAL FAT (4G SATURATED), 2G FIBER, 254MG CHOLESTEROL, 690MG SODIUM.

Leftover Revamp: To make **Turkey Pitas with Cucumber Salad**, combine **1 cup plain fat-free Greek yogurt** and **½ seedless cucumber,** peeled and finely chopped, in medium bowl; stir in **1 tablespoon lemon juice; 1 small clove garlic,** pressed; **reserved herb mixture;** and ⅛ teaspoon salt. Shred reserved turkey into chunks. Place in medium microwave-safe bowl; microwave on High 2 minutes. Toss **12 ounces ripe tomatoes,** chopped; **½ cucumber,** finely chopped; **½ small red onion,** finely chopped; **1 tablespoon fresh lemon juice; 2 teaspoons olive oil;** and ¼ teaspoon each salt and **pepper** in large bowl. Toast **4 pitas;** fill with turkey, cucumber salad, yogurt, and ⅓ **cup feta.** Serves 4.

EACH SERVING: ABOUT 490 CALORIES, 46G PROTEIN, 43G CARBOHYDRATE, 14G TOTAL FAT (5G SATURATED), 3G FIBER, 107MG CHOLESTEROL, 985 MG SODIUM.

PASTA

Southwestern
CHICKEN STEW

Bring the flavors of the Southwest to your dinner table with this rich and spicy chicken stew. Make sure to use "thin spaghetti" as opposed to angel hair or spaghettini; each of those is too thin and will get overcooked and mushy.

ACTIVE TIME: 15 MINUTES   **COOKING TIME:** 4 HOURS   **MAKES:** 8 MAIN-DISH SERVINGS

1   can (28 ounces) fire-roasted tomatoes

2   green onions, trimmed and cut into thirds, plus 2 green onions, thinly sliced, for garnish

2   chipotle chiles in adobo sauce

2   tablespoons adobo sauce

2   cloves garlic, peeled

2   teaspoons chili powder

1   teaspoon ground cumin

salt

1¼ pounds skinless, boneless chicken breast halves

2   cups chicken broth

½   cup water

1   pound thin spaghetti, broken into thirds

1½ cups finely shredded Monterey Jack cheese

cilantro leaves, for garnish

1 In blender, puree tomatoes, onions, chipotles, adobo sauce, garlic, chili powder, cumin, and 1 teaspoon salt until smooth. Transfer to 6- to 7-quart slow cooker bowl. Arrange chicken on top (do not submerge). Cover with lid; cook on Low 3½ hours or until chicken is cooked (165°F).

2 Transfer chicken to cutting board. In measuring cup, combine broth, water, and ¼ teaspoon salt. Microwave on high 1 minute; add to slow cooker. Add spaghetti, pushing down to fully submerge. Cover with lid; cook on Low 30 to 45 minutes, testing after 30 minutes, or until pasta is al dente and most of liquid has been absorbed, stirring once.

3 While pasta cooks, pull chicken into chunks. Once pasta is cooked, return chicken to bowl, tossing to combine. To serve, top with cheese, sliced green onions, and cilantro.

EACH SERVING: ABOUT 410 CALORIES, 29G PROTEIN, 50G CARBOHYDRATE, 10G TOTAL FAT (4G SATURATED), 4G FIBER, 50MG CHOLESTEROL, 1,120MG SODIUM.

Butternut Squash Barley Risotto
(page 110)

5

Vegetarian & Sides

Everyone knows the drill: Incorporating meatless meals into your weekly menu plan reduces grocery cost while also providing a slew of health benefits. And yet, it's not always easy to release meat from its center-stage power. That's where this chapter lends a hand—to show off other avenues for protein-packed entrees.

Dial up the bean factor with Potato and Garbanzo Bean Stew or White Chili with Black Beans. There's a multitude of legume love with Lentil Stew with Butternut Squash and Lentil and Cauliflower Curry. Stocking the pantry with staples, along with having a few starchy vegetables on hand, can make these your go-to dishes in a recipe pinch. Also, don't forget to lean on the slow cooker for a little side dish glory with succulent Boston Baked Beans and fluffy Slow Cooker Stuffing worthy of more than just holiday meals.

SLOW COOKER **Stuffing**

A make-ahead tip—toast bread, cool, break into pieces, and store in a plastic bag at room temperature up to 3 days prior to making the recipe.

ACTIVE TIME: 30 MINUTES   **COOKING TIME:** 6 HOURS   **MAKES:** ABOUT 8 CUPS

1   loaf (16 ounces) sliced firm white bread

5   stalks celery, cut into ½-inch pieces

1   large onion (12 ounces), coarsely chopped

½   cup trans-fat free margarine or butter (1 stick), sliced

½   cup loosely packed fresh sage leaves, chopped

salt and ground black pepper

1   small bunch parsley with stems, chopped (about ¾ cup)

3   firm pears, such as Bosc or Anjou (8 ounces each), peeled, cored, and cut into ¾-inch chunks

1   Preheat oven to 400°F. Divide bread between 2 large cookie sheets. Place cookie sheets on 2 oven racks and toast 20 to 25 minutes or until deep golden brown, rotating pans between upper and lower racks halfway through roasting and turning slices over once. Transfer toast to wire racks to cool.

2   Break toast into about 1-inch pieces. Place celery, onion, margarine or butter, sage, 1 teaspoon salt, ¼ teaspoon pepper, and ½ cup parsley (wrap and refrigerate remaining parsley to add to stuffing later) in bottom of 5-quart slow cooker bowl; toss to combine. Top with toast, then pears. Cover slow cooker with lid and cook on Low setting 5½ to 6 hours or until toast is moist.

3   Transfer stuffing to large serving bowl. Toss with remaining parsley to serve.

. . . .

EACH ½ CUP: ABOUT 155 CALORIES, 3G PROTEIN, 21G CARBOHYDRATE, 7G TOTAL FAT (1G SATURATED), 0MG CHOLESTEROL, 385MG SODIUM.

Lentil Stew
WITH BUTTERNUT SQUASH

This comforting, fiber-packed Italian favorite showcases rustic winter ingredients. Rich in vitamins A and C, butternut squash adds a subtle sweetness to this hearty stew.

ACTIVE TIME: 20 MINUTES   **COOKING TIME:** 8 HOURS   **MAKES:** 8 MAIN-DISH SERVINGS

3   large stalks celery, cut into ¼-inch thick slices

1   large onion (12 ounces), chopped

1   large butternut squash (2½ pounds), peeled, seeded, and cut into 1-inch chunks

1   bag (1 pound) brown lentils

4   cups water

1   can (14 to 14½ ounces) vegetable broth

½   teaspoon dried rosemary

salt and ground black pepper

1   ounce Parmesan or Romano cheese, shaved with vegetable peeler

¼   cup loosely packed fresh parsley leaves, chopped, to garnish

1 In 4½- to 6-quart slow cooker bowl, combine celery, onion, squash, lentils, water, broth, rosemary, ¾ teaspoon salt, and ¼ teaspoon ground black pepper. Cover slow cooker with lid, and cook on Low setting 8 hours.

2 To serve, spoon lentil stew into serving bowls; top with Parmesan or Romano shavings, and sprinkle with chopped parsley.

EACH SERVING: ABOUT 285 CALORIES, 20G PROTEIN, 51G CARBOHYDRATE, 2G TOTAL FAT (1G SATURATED), 20G FIBER, 3MG CHOLESTEROL, 420MG SODIUM.

BUTTERNUT SQUASH
Barley Risotto

This creamy, comforting dish is healthy, too. Full of fiber and essential nutrients, this barley-based risotto is just as delicious and satisfying as the rice-based original. To recycle risotto into a time-smart supper of Risotto Cakes with Tomato Salad on the next page, save ⅓ of the risotto to a container; refrigerate up to 3 days.

ACTIVE TIME: 15 MINUTES   **COOKING TIME:** 4 HOURS   **MAKES:** 8 MAIN-DISH SERVINGS

- 2 tablespoons trans-fat free margarine or butter
- 2 shallots, thinly sliced
- 2 sprigs fresh thyme
- 2 cups pearl barley
- 4 cups low-sodium chicken or vegetable broth
- 2 cups water
- 1 large butternut squash (2½ pounds), peeled and seeded, cut into ½-inch cubes

salt and ground black pepper

- 1 ounce Parmesan cheese, grated (⅔ cup)
- 2 tablespoons chopped fresh flat-leaf parsley leaves, for garnish

1 In 12-inch skillet, melt 1 tablespoon margarine or butter over medium-high heat. Add shallots and cook 2 minutes or until golden, stirring often. Add thyme; cook 30 seconds. Add barley and cook 2 minutes or until toasted and golden, stirring often.

2 Transfer to 6-quart slow cooker bowl, along with broth, water, squash, and ½ teaspoon salt. Cover and cook on High 3½ to 4 hours or until liquid is absorbed and squash is tender.

3 Uncover; discard thyme. Add Parmesan, remaining tablespoon margarine, 1 teaspoon salt, and ¼ teaspoon ground black pepper. Gently stir until margarine and Parmesan melt. Transfer mixture to serving dishes and garnish with parsley.

EACH SERVING: ABOUT 235 CALORIES, 7G PROTEIN, 45G CARBOHYDRATE, 4G TOTAL FAT (1G SATURATED), 10G FIBER, 3MG CHOLESTEROL, 670MG SODIUM.

Leftover Revamp: To make **Risotto Cakes with Tomato Salad**, combine **2¼ pounds ripe tomatoes**, seeded and chopped; **1 small clove garlic**, pressed; **1 tablespoon balsamic vinegar**; **1 tablespoon olive oil**; **⅛ teaspoon salt**; and **⅛ teaspoon ground black pepper** in large bowl. Stir in **¼ cup fresh basil leaves**, torn. Combine **reserved risotto, 1 large egg; ¼ cup grated Pecorino Romano cheese; ¼ cup fresh basil leaves**, finely chopped; and **¼ teaspoon ground black pepper** in another large bowl. Using a ⅓-cup measuring cup, form mixture into 12 patties (¾-inch thick). Heat **1 teaspoon vegetable oil** in 12-inch nonstick skillet, on medium 1 minute. Add half of patties. Cook 8 minutes or until golden brown. Carefully turn over and cook 4 minutes or until golden brown. Repeat with remaining mixture, cooking each side 4 minutes. Serve with tomato salad. Serves 6.

EACH SERVING: ABOUT 220 CALORIES, 8G PROTEIN, 29G CARBOHYDRATE, 9G TOTAL FAT (2G SATURATED), 7G FIBER, 39MG CHOLESTEROL, 490MG SODIUM.

BOSTON
Baked Beans

This delicious side dish is traditionally made with navy or pea beans, molasses, and brown sugar and is baked for hours until the beans are tender and the sauce is syrupy.

ACTIVE TIME: 10 MINUTES   **COOKING TIME:** 14 HOURS, PLUS SOAKING   **MAKES:** 10 SIDE-DISH SERVINGS

1   pound dry small white beans

3½ cups water

1   medium onion (6 to 8 ounces), chopped

4   slices bacon, chopped

¼   cup light (mild) molasses

¼   cup packed dark brown sugar

2   teaspoons dry mustard

¼   teaspoon ground black pepper

⅛   teaspoon ground cloves

1½ teaspoons salt

1   Rinse beans with cold running water and discard any stones or shriveled beans. In large bowl, place beans and enough water to cover by 2 inches. Cover and let stand at room temperature overnight. (Or, in 6-quart saucepot, place beans and enough water to cover by 2 inches. Heat to boiling over high heat; cook 2 minutes. Remove from heat; cover and let stand 1 hour.) Drain and rinse beans.

2   In 4½- to 5½-quart slow cooker pot, stir 3½ cups water with beans and remaining ingredients except salt, until blended.

3   Cover slow cooker with lid and cook beans on Low about 14 hours or until beans are tender and sauce is syrupy. Stir salt into bean mixture before serving.

EACH SERVING: ABOUT 285 CALORIES, 12G PROTEIN, 39G CARBOHYDRATE, 9G TOTAL FAT (3G SATURATED), 5G FIBER, 10MG CHOLESTEROL, 475MG SODIUM.

Curried Lentils
WITH SWEET POTATO

An Indian-inspired vegetarian stew that is delicious and easy to make.
Lentils are available in a variety of colors: brown, red and yellow, all but
red ones hold their shape in the slow cooker.

ACTIVE TIME: 20 MINUTES   **COOKING TIME:** 10 HOURS ON LOW OR 6 HOURS ON HIGH
MAKES: 6 MAIN-DISH SERVINGS

2   teaspoons vegetable oil

1   medium shallot, sliced

2   cloves garlic crushed with press

1   tablespoon peeled, minced fresh ginger

2   teaspoons curry powder

1   teaspoon ground cumin

salt

1   large sweet potato, peeled and cut into
    1-inch chunks

2   cups dried lentils, rinsed

4   cups vegetable broth

2   tablespoons tomato paste

5   ounces baby spinach

basmati rice, for serving (optional)

cilantro leaves, for garnish (optional)

fat-free yogurt, for garnish (optional)

1 In 12-inch skillet, heat vegetable oil on
medium. Add shallots, garlic, ginger,
curry powder, cumin, and ¼ teaspoon salt.
Cook 1 to 3 minutes or until slightly softened,
stirring frequently. Transfer to 6- to 7-quart slow
cooker bowl.

2 To slow cooker bowl, add sweet potatoes, then
lentils, vegetable broth, and tomato paste. Cover
and cook 9 to 10 hours on Low or 6 hours on
High, or until lentils are tender.

3 To serve, into slow cooker bowl, stir in baby
spinach and ½ teaspoon salt until spinach is
wilted. Serve with cooked basmati rice. Garnish
with fresh cilantro leaves and dollop of fat-free
yogurt, if desired.

EACH SERVING: ABOUT 290 CALORIES, 18G PROTEIN,
52G CARBOHYDRATE, 3G TOTAL FAT (0G SATURATED),
17G FIBER, 0MG CHOLESTEROL, 610MG SODIUM.

Secrets of Veggie Success

No one loves mushy mystery vegetables.
Here's where to place 'em to preserve their flavor and texture.

1. BOTTOM LAYER

Position the densest, toughest veggies at the bottom of the cooker, where temps are highest.

Think: Turnips, parsnips, cabbage, potatoes, sweet potatoes, winter squash

2. MIDDLE LAYER

The middle is the go-to zone for semi-hardy veggies: They'll cook through there without going soft.

Think: Fennel, carrots, green beans, bell peppers, celery

3. TOP LAYER

These more delicate veggies can't hold up through hours of heat, so add them in the last 30 minutes of cooking.

Think: Broccoli, fresh herbs, spinach, peas, zucchini

POTATO AND GARBANZO
Bean Stew

Adding a fried or poached egg on top of this stew provides an extra jolt of protein along with the rich silkiness of the broken yolk.

ACTIVE TIME: 15 MINUTES   **COOKING TIME:** 5 HOURS   **MAKES:** 4 MAIN-DISH SERVINGS

1¼ pounds Yukon gold potatoes, cut into 1-inch chunks

3   medium carrots, peeled and chopped

1   can (15 ounces) garbanzo beans, drained

1   pound zucchini, cut into 1-inch chunks

1   cup water

2   teaspoons fennel seeds

1   teaspoon coriander

salt and gound black pepper

½   teaspoon cinnamon

1   lemon, cut into quarters

1   cup frozen peas

4   fried or poached eggs

chopped fresh mint, for serving

1 In 6- or 7-quart slow cooker bowl, layer potatoes, carrots, garbanzo beans, and zucchini.

2 In a small bowl, whisk together water, fennel seeds, coriander, 1 teaspoon salt, cinnamon, and ½ teaspoon pepper; pour over vegetables. Top with lemon quarters. Cover and cook on High 5 hours.

3 Ten minutes before serving, add peas to cooker and cover. To serve, remove and discard lemon. Divide stew among 4 bowls. Top each with fried or poached egg and mint.

....

EACH SERVING: ABOUT 365 CALORIES, 19G PROTEIN, 56G CARBOHYDRATE, 7G TOTAL FAT (2G SATURATED), 7G FIBER, 0MG CHOLESTEROL, 940MG SODIUM.

AFRICAN
Sweet Potato–Peanut Stew

An unlikely but delicious combo, peanut butter and tomatoes create the base for this African dish.

ACTIVE TIME: 25 MINUTES   **COOKING TIME:** 10 HOURS ON LOW OR 5 HOURS ON HIGH
MAKES: 6 MAIN-DISH SERVINGS

3   cloves garlic

2   cups loosely packed fresh cilantro leaves and stems

1   can (28 ounces) diced tomatoes

½   cup creamy or chunky peanut butter

2   teaspoons ground cumin

½   teaspoon ground cinnamon

¼   teaspoon ground red pepper (cayenne)

salt

1   cup water

3   pounds sweet potatoes, peeled and cut into 2-inch chunks

1   can (15 to 19 ounces) garbanzo beans, rinsed and drained

1   package (16 ounces) frozen whole or cut green beans

1   In blender or food processor with knife blade attached, blend garlic, cilantro, tomatoes with their juice, peanut butter, cumin, cinnamon, ground red pepper, and ¾ teaspoon salt until pureed.

2   Into 4½- to 6-quart slow cooker bowl, pour peanut-butter mixture; stir in water. Add sweet potatoes and garbanzo beans; stir to combine. Cover slow cooker with lid and cook on Low setting 8 to 10 hours or on High setting 4 to 5 hours, or until potatoes are very tender.

3   About 10 minutes before sweet potato mixture is done, cook green beans as label directs. Gently stir green beans into stew.

EACH SERVING: ABOUT 495 CALORIES, 16G PROTEIN, 83G CARBOHYDRATE, 13G TOTAL FAT (3G SATURATED), 12G FIBER, 0MG CHOLESTEROL, 1,105MG SODIUM.

LENTIL AND CAULIFLOWER
Curry

Ginger, warm spices, and coconut milk add satisfying depth to this Indian favorite. Cauliflower is high in Vitamin C and a good source of iron.

ACTIVE TIME: 10 MINUTES   **COOKING TIME:** ABOUT 8 HOURS ON LOW OR 5 HOURS ON HIGH
MAKES: 6 MAIN-DISH SERVINGS

2   medium shallots, quartered

1   can (6 ounces) tomato paste

1   jalapeño chile, stemmed

4   slices (thick) peeled ginger

2   cloves garlic, peeled

2   teaspoons ground cumin

2   teaspoons ground coriander

salt and ground black pepper

2   cups vegetable broth

1½ cups lentils, rinsed

1   can (15 ounces) light coconut milk

1   cup water

3   cups large cauliflower flowerets

1   cup frozen peas, thawed

1   tablespoon fresh lime juice (from about 2 limes)

cooked basmati rice, for serving

⅓   cup chopped shelled unsalted pistachios, for garnish

1   In food processor, pulse shallots, tomato paste, jalapeño, ginger, garlic, cumin, coriander, and ½ teaspoon each salt and black pepper until mostly smooth; transfer to 7- to 8-quart slow cooker bowl.

2   To same slow cooker bowl, add broth, lentils, coconut milk, and water, stirring to combine. Place cauliflower on top. Cover with lid and cook on Low 8 hours or on High 5 hours , or until lentils are tender.

3   Into slow cooker bowl, stir peas, lime juice, and ¼ teaspoon salt. Serve over rice; garnish with pistachios.

EACH SERVING: ABOUT 355 CALORIES, 19G PROTEIN, 48G CARBOHYDRATE, 9G TOTAL FAT (5G SATURATED), 20G FIBER, 0MG CHOLESTEROL, 670MG SODIUM.

White Chili
WITH BLACK BEANS

Protein-rich lentils star in this spin on chili—
delicious and comforting for a cold winter day.

ACTIVE TIME: 20 MINUTES   COOKING TIME: 10 HOURS ON LOW OR 6 HOURS ON HIGH
MAKES: 8 MAIN-DISH SERVINGS

2   teaspoons vegetable oil

1   medium onion (6 to 8 ounces), chopped

2   cloves garlic, chopped

1   teaspoon chili powder

salt

1   package (20 ounces) peeled butternut squash chunks, cut into quarters

1   can (15 ounces) low-sodium black beans, rinsed and drained

2   cups dried lentils, rinsed

5   cups low-sodium vegetable broth

1   jar (16 ounces) salsa verde (green salsa)

1   can (4 ounces) chopped green chiles

shredded Cheddar cheese, if desired, for serving

lime wedges, if desired, for serving

1   In 12-inch skillet, heat vegetable oil on medium. Add onion, garlic, chili powder, and ¼ teaspoon salt. Cook 1 to 3 minutes or until slightly softened, stirring frequently. Transfer to 6- to 7-quart slow cooker bowl.

2   To slow cooker bowl, add butternut squash, black beans, lentils, broth, salsa verde, and chopped green chiles.

3   Cover and cook 9 to 10 hours on Low or 6 hours on High, or until lentils are tender. Serve with shredded Cheddar cheese and lime wedges, if desired.

EACH SERVING (WITHOUT CHEESE): ABOUT 285 CALO-RIES, 17G PROTEIN, 50G CARBOHYDRATE, 3G TOTAL FAT (0G SATURATED), 15G FIBER, 0MG CHOLESTEROL, 885MG SODIUM.

Index

Note: Page numbers in italics indicate photos of recipes located separately from respective recipes.

Photography Credits

Metric Conversion Charts

The recipes that appear in this cookbook use the standard United States method for measuring liquid and dry or solid ingredients (teaspoons, tablespoons, and cups). The information on this chart is provided to help cooks outside the U.S. successfully use these recipes. All equivalents are approximate.

METRIC EQUIVALENTS FOR DIFFERENT TYPES OF INGREDIENTS

STANDARD CUP (e.g. flour)	FINE POWDER (e.g. rice)	GRAIN (e.g. sugar)	GRANULAR (e.g. butter)	LIQUID SOLIDS (e.g. milk)	LIQUID
¾	105 g	113 g	143 g	150 g	180 ml
⅔	93 g	100 g	125 g	133 g	160 ml
½	70 g	75 g	95 g	100 g	120 ml
⅓	47 g	50 g	63 g	67 g	80 ml
¼	35 g	38 g	48 g	50 g	60 ml
⅛	18 g	19 g	24 g	25 g	30 ml

USEFUL EQUIVALENTS FOR LIQUID INGREDIENTS BY VOLUME

¼ tsp	=						1 ml
½ tsp	=						2 ml
1 tsp	=						5 ml
3 tsp	=	1 tbls	=		½ fl oz	=	15 ml
		2 tbls	=	⅛ cup	1 fl oz	=	30 ml
		4 tbls	=	¼ cup	2 fl oz	=	60 ml
		5⅓ tbls	=	⅓ cup	3 fl oz	=	80 ml
		8 tbls	=	½ cup	4 fl oz	=	120 ml
		10⅔ tbls	=	⅔ cup	5 fl oz	=	160 ml
		12 tbls	=	¾ cup	6 fl oz	=	180 ml
		16 tbls	=	1 cup	8 fl oz	=	240 ml
		1 pt	=	2 cups	16 fl oz	=	480 ml
		1 qt	=	4 cups	32 fl oz	=	960 ml
					33 fl oz	=	1000 ml = 1 L

USEFUL EQUIVALENTS FOR DRY INGREDIENTS BY WEIGHT

(To convert ounces to grams, multiply the number of ounces by 30.)

1 oz	=	¹⁄₁₆ lb	=	30 g
2 oz	=	¼ lb	=	120 g
4 oz	=	½ lb	=	240 g
8 oz	=	¾ lb	=	360 g
16 oz	=	1 lb	=	480 g

USEFUL EQUIVALENTS FOR COOKING/OVEN TEMPERATURES

	Fahrenheit	Celsius	Gas Mark
Freeze Water	32° F	0° C	
Room Temperature	68° F	20° C	
Boil Water	212° F	100° C	
Bake	325° F	160° C	3
	350° F	180° C	4
	375° F	190° C	5
	400° F	200° C	6
	425° F	220° C	7
	450° F	230° C	8
Broil			Grill

USEFUL EQUIVALENTS LENGTH

(To convert inches to centimeters, multiply the number of inches by 2.5.)

1 in	=		2.5 cm	
6 in	=	½ ft =	15 cm	
12 in	=	1 ft =	30 cm	
36 in	=	3 ft = 1 yd =	90 cm	
40 in	=		100 cm	= 1 m

THE GOOD HOUSEKEEPING
TRIPLE-TEST PROMISE

At *Good Housekeeping*, we want to make sure that every recipe we print works in any oven, with any brand of ingredient, no matter what. That's why, in our test kitchens at the **Good Housekeeping Research Institute**, we go all out: We test each recipe at least three times—and, often, several more times after that.

When a recipe is first developed, one member of our team prepares the dish, and we judge it on these criteria: It must be **delicious**, **family-friendly**, **healthy**, and **easy to make**.

1   The recipe is then tested several more times to fine-tune the flavor and ease of preparation, always by the same team member, using the same equipment.

2   Next, another team member follows the recipe as written, **varying the brands of ingredients** and **kinds of equipment**. Even the types of stoves we use are changed.

3   A third team member repeats the whole process **using yet another set of equipment** and **alternative ingredients**. By the time the recipes appear on these pages, they are guaranteed to work in any kitchen, including yours. **We promise**.